A THOUSAND CLOWNS

A New Comedy

by HERB GARDNER

RANDOM HOUSE
NEW YORK

A Thousand Clowns

This play,

and as many cantaloupes as I can get my hands on,

is for Rita.

A Thousand Clowns *was first presented by Fred Coe and Arthur Cantor at the Eugene O'Neill Theatre, New York City, April 5, 1962, with the following cast:*

(IN ORDER OF APPEARANCE)

Nick Burns	Barry Gordon
Murray Burns	Jason Robards, Jr.
Albert Amundson	William Daniels
Sandra Markowitz	Sandy Dennis
Arnold Burns	A. Larry Haines
Leo Herman	Gene Saks

Directed by Fred Coe

Scenery designed and lighted by George Jenkins

Costumes by Ruth Morley

ACT ONE

ACT ONE

In complete darkness, before the curtain goes up, we hear the voice of Chuckles the Chipmunk.

CHUCKLES' VOICE (*Intimately, softly*)   Goshes and gollygoods, kidderoonies; now what're all us Chippermunkies gonna play first this fine mornin'?

CHORUS OF KIDS   Gonna play Chuckle-Chip Dancing.

CHUCKLES' VOICE   And with who?

CHORUS OF KIDS   With you!

CHUCKLES' VOICE (*Louder*)   And who is me?

CHORUS OF KIDS (*Screaming*)   Chuckles the Chippermunkie! Rayyyyyyyyyyyyyyyy.

The curtain goes up on this last screaming syllable, revealing MURRAY BURNS' *one-room apartment. The voices of Chuckles and the kids continue but are now coming from an ancient table-model T.V. set at the left. The set is facing away from the audience and is being watched by* NICHOLAS BURNS, *a twelve-year-old. The apartment is on the second floor of a brownstone on the lower West Side of Manhattan. It consists of one large, high-ceilinged room in which borrowed furniture rambles in no meaningful arrangement—some gaudy, some impractical, no matching pieces. It is obvious from* MURRAY BURNS' *apartment that he is a collector, though it is not entirely clear just what he is a collector of. All about the room, on the floor, on the coffee table, on dresser tops, is* MURRAY's *collection: eighteen broken radios, some with interesting cathedral-style cabinets; over two dozen elaborately disabled clocks of different sizes, some of them on the wall; parts of eight Victrolas, mostly cabinets; a variety of hats, including a Prussian helmet and a deerstalker; a pirate pistol; a bugle; a megaphone; and stacks of magazines and books. It is somehow, though, a very comfort-able-looking apartment. There is an alcove at the left, with a small bed, a child's desk and some bookshelves. This is* NICK's *part of the place and it is very neat, ordered, organized, seem-ing almost to have nothing to do with the main room. There is a bathroom door at left below the small alcove. Right of the alcove are three large windows and a built-in window seat. A closed venetian blind covers all three windows. At center is a large, comfortable rumpled bed with an elaborate wooden headboard running up the wall almost to the ceiling. The head-board is loaded with clocks, radios, and two lamps. At right is the entrance door to the apartment. To the left of the door are two large office-style filing cabinets in which* MURRAY *keeps some of his clothes, and to the right is a bureau covered with knickknacks on which* MURRAY's *hats are hung. Downstage right is the kitchen door; to the left of it is a desk buried under papers, and built-in bookshelves stuffed with a jumble of books and nonsense. There is a closet to the left of the desk. A Morris chair and an armless swivel chair are on either side of a small table at right and there is a brightly colored beach chair at left in front of the windows.*

At rise: It is eight-thirty on a Monday morning; it is rather dark, the only real light is a scattered haze from the television set. The chorus of kids is now singing the "Chuckles Song." NICK *watches expressionlessly.*

CHORUS OF KIDS (*Singing*) Who's whitcha at—eight-thirty?
Who's face is so—so dirty?
Who's sparky—who's spunky?
Chip, Chip, Chip, Chip—Chippermunkie!

NICK (*Quietly*) Oh, this is terrible. This is rotten.

CHORUS OF KIDS   Who's always good—for funnin'?
  Whose scooter-bike—keeps runnin'?
        (MURRAY *enters from the kitchen carrying a cup of cof-
        fee; he is in his mid-thirties. He is wearing shorts and
        an undershirt and is not quite awake yet*)

MURRAY (*Walking across to the bed*)   Get those kids outa
  here. (*Sits on the bed*)   Nick, what'd I tell you about bringing your friends in here this early in the morning?

NICK   It's not my friends; it's the T.V.

MURRAY   Play with your friends outside. Get those kids out of
  here. (NICK *turns the set off*. MURRAY *looks over at the front
  door, waves at it and shouts*)   Good. And none of you kids
  come back here till this afternoon.

NICK   It wasn't my friends. It was Chuckles the Chipmunk.

MURRAY (*Sleepily*)   That's very comforting.

NICK (*Brings a pack of cigarettes to* MURRAY)   Boy, it's a terrible program now. It was a much better show when you
  were writing it.

MURRAY   When Sandburg and Faulkner quit, I quit. What
  kind of a day is it outside?

NICK (*Going to the kitchen*)   It's a Monday.

MURRAY   I mean warm or cold or sunny is what I mean.

NICK   I haven't been outside yet.

5

MURRAY (*He pulls the blind up revealing the windows; there is no change whatever in the lighting, the room remains dark. The windows have no view other than the gray blank wall of the building a few feet opposite*) Ah, light. (*He leans out of the window, cranes his head around to look up at the sky*) Can't see a thing. Not a thing. (*Pulls his head back in*) No matter what time of day or what season, we got a permanent fixture out there; twilight in February.

NICK (*Bringing the coffee pot out of the kitchen and filling* MURRAY's *cup*) You better call the weather record like always.

MURRAY One morning I'll wake up and that damn building'll have fallen down into Seventh Avenue so I can see the weather. (*Picks up the phone; dialing*) Using a machine to call up another machine. I do not enjoy the company of ghosts. (*Into the phone*) Hello, Weather Lady! Well, I'm just fine, and how is your nasal little self this morning? What's the weather? Uh-huh. That high? And the wind, which way does the wind blow this morning? Ah, good. Uh-huh, all the way to East Point and Block Island. Humidity? Very decent. Whoops, oh, there you go again. You simply *must* learn not to repeat yourself. I keep telling you every morning that once is enough. You'll never learn. (*Hangs up*) Women seldom sense when they have become boring. (*Goes to the window again, leans out, raises his voice, shouting out of the window*) Neighbors, I have an announcement for you. I have *never seen* such a collection of dirty windows. Now I want to see you all out there on the fire escape with your Mr. Clean bottles, and let's snap it up . . .

NICK Gee, Murray, you gotta shout like that every morning?

MURRAY It clears my head. (*After glancing around clock-filled apartment*) What time is it?

NICK It's eight-forty.

MURRAY Well, what're you doing here? Why aren't you in school?

NICK It's a holiday. It's Irving R. Feldman's birthday, like you said.

MURRAY Irving R. Feldman's birthday is my own personal national holiday. I did not open it up for the public. He is proprietor of perhaps the most distinguished kosher delicatessen in this neighborhood and as such I hold the day of his birth in reverence.

NICK You said you weren't going to look for work today because it was Irving R. Feldman's birthday, so I figured I would celebrate too, a little.

MURRAY Don't kid *me*, Nick, you know you're supposed to be in school. I thought you *liked* that damn genius' school— why the hell—

NICK Well, I figured I'd better stay home today till you got up. (*Hesitantly*) There's something I gotta discuss with you. See, because it's this special school for big brains they watch you and take notes and make reports and smile at you a lot. And there's this psychologist who talks to you every week, each kid separately. He's the biggest smiler they got up there.

MURRAY Because you got brains they figure you're nuts.

NICK Anyway, we had Show and Tell time in Mrs. Zimmerman's class on Monday; and each kid in the class is supposed to tell about some trip he took and show pictures. Well, y'remember when I made you take me with you to the El Bambino Club over on Fifty-second?

MURRAY Nick . . . you showed and you told.

NICK Well, it turned out they're very square up at the Revere School. And sometimes in class, when we have our Wednesday Free-Association-Talk Period, I sometimes quote you on different opinions . . .

MURRAY That wasn't a good idea.

NICK Well, I didn't know they were such nervous people there. Murray, they're very nervous there. And then there was this composition I wrote in Creative Writing about the advantages of Unemployment Insurance.

MURRAY Why did you write about that?

NICK It was just on my mind. Then once they got my record out they started to notice what they call "significant data." Turns out they've been keeping this file on me for a long time, and checking with that Child Welfare place; same place you got those letters from.

MURRAY I never answer letters from large organizations.

8

NICK So, Murray . . . when they come over here, I figure we'd better . . .

MURRAY When they come over here?

NICK Yeah, this Child Welfare crowd, they want to take a look at our environment here.

MURRAY Oh, that's charming. Why didn't you tell me about this before, Nick?

NICK Well, y'know, the past coupla nights we couldn't get together.

MURRAY That was unavoidable. You know when I have a lot of work you stay up at Mrs. Myers'.

NICK (*Pointing at the dresser*) Murray; your work forgot her gloves last night.

MURRAY That's very bright.

NICK Anyway, for this Child Welfare crowd, I figure we better set up some kind of story before they get here.

MURRAY You make it sound like a vice raid.

NICK I mean, for one thing, you don't even have a job right now.

MURRAY Look, you want me to put up some kind of front when they get here? O.K., I will. Don't worry, kid. I'll snow 'em good.

9

NICK   I thought maybe you could at least look in the papers for a job, this morning before they get here. So we could tell them about your possibilities.

MURRAY   (*Without much conviction*)   I look every day.

NICK   Couldn't I just read you from the *Times* again like last week? While you get dressed?

MURRAY   O.K., read me from the paper.
    (*He starts to get dressed*)

NICK   And then, maybe, you'll take a shave?

MURRAY   All right, all right.

NICK   (*Picking up the* Times *from the swivel chair*)   This paper is three days old.

MURRAY   So what do you want me to do, bury it? Is it starting to rot or something? Read me from the paper.

NICK   But most of these jobs, somebody must have taken them. Look, I'll go down and get a newer—

MURRAY   We do *not* need a newer paper. All the really important jobs stay forever. Now start on the first page of Help-Wanted-Male and read me from the paper.

NICK   O.K. (*Puts on his glasses; reads aloud*)   "Administ, Exoppty. To ninety dollars." What's that?

MURRAY Administrative Assistant, excellent opportunity. Nothing. Keep reading.

NICK But ninety dollars would be ninety dollars more than nothing. Nothing is what you make now.

MURRAY Have you ever considered being the first twelve-year-old boy in space?

NICK But, ninety dollars . . .

MURRAY *You* go be an Administ, Exoppty. They *need* men like you. Read further.

NICK (*Reading from the paper*) "Versatile Junior, traffic manager, industrial representative organization. One hundred to one hundred twenty-five dollars. Call Mr. Shiffman."

MURRAY (*Picks up the cardboard from his shirt collar and talks into it*) Hello, Mr. Shiffman? I read your name in the New York *Times,* so I know you must be real. My name is Mandrake the Magician. I am a versatile Junior and I would like to manage your traffic for you. You see, sir, it has long been my ambition to work in a pointless job, with no future and a cretin like you as my boss . . .

NICK But, Murray, it says "one hundred twenty-five dollars," that's a lot of . . .

MURRAY Just read the ads. No editorial comment or personal recommendations. When I need your advice, I'll ask for it. Out of the mouths of babes comes drooling.

NICK You said that last week. Murray, you don't want a job is the whole thing.

MURRAY Would you just concentrate on being a child? Because I find your imitation of an adult hopelessly inadequate.

NICK You want to be your own boss, but the trouble with that is you don't pay yourself anything. (NICK *decides that what he has just said is very funny. He laughs*) Hey—you don't pay yourself anything—that's a good line—I gotta remember that.

MURRAY That's what *you* said last week.

NICK Look, Murray. (*He puts the paper down and stands up*) Can I speak to you man to man?

MURRAY That was cute about a year ago, buddy, but that line has got to go.

NICK (*Takes off his glasses*) Murray, I am upset. For me as an actual child the way you live in this house and we live is a dangerous thing for my later life when I become an actual person. An unemployed person like you are for so many months is bad for you as the person involved and is definitely bad for me who he lives with in the same house where the rent isn't paid for months sometimes. And I wish you would get a job, Murray. Please.
(MURRAY *tries to control himself but cannot hide his laughter; he sees that* NICK *is offended by this and tries to stop.* NICK *walks away from him, goes to his alcove*)

MURRAY (*Goes to* NICK *in the alcove*) Kid, I know. I'm sorry. You're right. You are. This *is* terrible.

NICK You're not kidding.

MURRAY Nick.

NICK Yeah?

MURRAY Nick, y'know when I said I was looking for work last week? (*Somewhat ashamed*) Well, I went to the movies. Every day. In the afternoon.

NICK *Murray,* you mean you really . . .

MURRAY Now don't give me any of that indignant crap. I happen to be admitting something to you, and it is bad enough I should have to discuss my adult problems with a grotesque cherub, without you giving me dirty looks on top of it. Swell crowd in the movies on a weekday working afternoon. Nobody sits next to anybody, everybody there figures that everybody else is a creep; and *all* of them are right. (*Suddenly smiling, taking* NICK's *arm, trying to change the subject*) Have you ever been to the top of the Empire State Building?

NICK Yes. Six times. With you. In November.

MURRAY Oh, really? Have you ever been to the Statue of Liberty?

NICK No.

MURRAY Today is Irving R. Feldman's birthday. We will go

to the top of the Statue of Liberty and watch the *Queen Elizabeth* come in, full of those tired, poor, huddled masses yearning to breath free.

NICK Murray, why did you go to the movies in the middle of the afternoon when you said you were looking for work?

MURRAY There's a window right in her navel, we will look out and see . . .

NICK What is it? Were you very tired, or what?

MURRAY (*Sits down in his chair*) See, last week I was going to check with Uncle Arnie and some of the other agents about writing for some of the new T.V. shows. I was on the subway, on my way there, and I got off at Forty-second Street and went to the movies. (*He leans back in his chair, lights a cigarette;* NICK *sits opposite him on the bed*) There are eleven movie houses on that street, Nick. It is Movieland. It breathes that seductive, carpety, minty air of the inside of movie houses. Almost as irresistible for me as pastrami. Now, there is the big question as you approach the box office, with the sun shining right down the middle of a working day, whether everybody going in is as embarrassed as you are. But once you are past the awkward stage, and have gotten your ticket torn by the old man inside, all doubts just go away. Because it is dark. And inside it is such a scene as to fracture the imagination of even a nut like yourself, Nick, because inside it is lovely and a little damp and nobody can see you, and the dialogue is falling like rain on a roof and you are sitting deep in front of a roaring, color, Cinemascope, stereophonic, nerve-cooling, heart-warming, spine-softening, perfect-happy-ending picture show and it is Peacefulville, U.S.A. There are men there with neat mustaches who have shaved, and shined their shoes and put on a tie even, to come and sit alone in the movies. And there are near-sighted cute pink ladies who eat secret caramels; and very old men who sleep; and the *ushers;* buddy, you are not kidding *these* boys. They know you are not there because you are waiting for a train, or you are on a vacation, or you work a night job. They know you are there to *see* the *movie.* It is the business and the purpose of your day, and these boys give you their sneaky smile to show you that they know. (*Depressed by his own words; quietly, almost to himself*) Now the moral question for me here, is this: When one is faced with life in the bare-assed, job-hunting raw on the one hand, and eleven fifty-cent double features on the other, what is the mature, sensible, and mentally healthy step to take?

(*He is slumped in his chair now*)

NICK (*Seeing* MURRAY's *depression; softly, with concern*) What's wrong, Murray?

MURRAY (*Walks slowly to the window, leans against the wall, looks sadly out of the window; speaks quietly*) I don't know. I'm not sure.

NICK Hey, Murray, you all right . . . ? (*He goes to* MURRAY, *touches his arm. Then smiling suddenly in an attempt to cheer him*) Murray, let's go to the Statue of Liberty.

(MURRAY *turns, laughs in agreement, and* NICK *starts for his jacket while* MURRAY *puts his binoculars around his neck and begins putting on his jacket. The doorbell rings.* NICK *looks at* MURRAY, *then goes to answer it.* NICK

15

is holding the front door only part-way open, hesitating to let in two people we now see standing outside in the hall. They are ALBERT AMUNDSON *and* SANDRA MARKOWITZ. ALBERT, *graduate of N.Y.U.'s School of Social Work, is a middle-aged man of twenty-eight.* SANDRA, *though a pretty girl of twenty-five, wears clothes obviously more suited to a much older woman.* ALBERT *carries a small briefcase and* SANDRA *carries two manila file envelopes and a gigantic handbag*)

ALBERT   Hello, young man, I am Mr. Amundson, this is Miss Markowitz. We would like to speak to your uncle.

NICK   (*Still not opening the door all the way*)   Well, I don't know if . . .

ALBERT   Isn't he in?

MURRAY   Hello.

ALBERT   How do you do, Mr. Burns. Miss Markowitz and I are a Social Service unit assigned to the New York Bureau of Child Welfare. We have been asked by the Bureau to— May we come in?

MURRAY   Certainly.
(NICK *opens the door all the way, letting them both into the main room*)

ALBERT   We, Miss Markowitz and I, have been asked by the B.C.W. to investigate and examine certain pupils of the Revere School. There is certain information which the school and the city would like to have, regarding young Nicholas.

MURRAY Sit down, Miss Markowitz, please. Mr. Amundson. I'll just get rid of these things.

(MURRAY *takes pants, shirts, a bugle, a clock, a yoyo, a half-empty bag of peanuts and an ash tray off the chairs, and with one sweeping movement puts all of them on the bed. The three of them take seats around the coffee table,* NICK *standing nervously off to one side*)

ALBERT I'd like to explain just why we are here, Mr. Burns . . .

NICK Would anybody like some coffee?

ALBERT Why, thank you, Nicholas. Miss Markowitz?

SANDRA Yes, thank you.

NICK (*Whispering to* MURRAY *on his way to the kitchen*) Watch it.

ALBERT (*Smiling politely*) It might be best, Mr. Burns, for the child, if perhaps you sent him downstairs to play or something, while we have our discussion. Your case is . . .

MURRAY Our "case." I had no idea we were a "case."

ALBERT We do have a file on certain students at Revere.

MURRAY So we're on file somewhere. Are we a great, big, fat file, or a li'l teeny file?

ALBERT Due to the fact that you have chosen not to answer our letters and several of our phone calls, there are many areas in which the file is incomplete, several questions— Mr. Burns, it might be better if the child went outside . . .

MURRAY You gonna talk dirty?

ALBERT It would be more advisable for the child not to be present, since Miss Markowitz, who will be discussing the psychological area . . . that is, we will be discussing certain matters which . . .

NICK (*From the kitchen*) Cream and sugar for everybody?

ALBERT (*To the kitchen*) Yes, Nicholas. (*To* MURRAY *again*) Mr. Burns, it's going to be awkward, with the child present, to . . .

MURRAY (*To* SANDRA) Miss Markowitz, may I know your first name?

SANDRA Sandra.

MURRAY And you are the psychologist part of this team, Sandy?

SANDRA That's right, Mr. Burns.

MURRAY (*To* ALBERT) And you, I take it, are the brawn of the outfit?

ALBERT Perhaps I should explain, Mr. Burns, that the Social Service teams which serve Revere School are a carefully planned balance of Social Case Worker, such as myself, and Psychological Social Worker, such as Miss Markowitz, or, actually, *Dr.* Markowitz. (NICK *enters from the kitchen with four cups, gives one each to* ALBERT, SANDRA, MURRAY; *keeps one for himself*) Mr. Burns, it is not easy to define those elements, those influences and problems which go into the make-up of a young boy.

MURRAY   I thought it was just frogs and snails and puppy dogs' tails.

ALBERT   (*Using once again his polite smile*)   I appreciate the informality with which you approach this meeting, Mr. Burns, but on the more serious side, if I may, Miss Markowitz and I have a few matters . . .

NICK   Is the coffee any good?

ALBERT   Yes, very good. Thank you, Nicholas.

SANDRA   Very nice, Nicholas. (*She sees the cup in* NICK's *hand, speaks with professional interest*)   Are you drinking coffee, Nicholas? Don't you think it would be better if . . .

NICK   No. Milk. I like to drink it from a cup.

MURRAY   (*To* SANDRA, *smiling*)   Now aren't you ashamed of yourself?

ALBERT   (*Taking a rather large file out of his briefcase*)   Now, to plunge right in here . . .

MURRAY   Sometimes I put his milk in a shot glass. Better for getting him to drink it than adding chocolate syrup.

SANDRA (*Firmly*) Mr. Burns, Mr. Amundson and I have several cases to examine today, and we would appreciate a certain amount of cooperation . . .

MURRAY (*To* NICK) East Bronx, Mosholu Parkway.

NICK (*Looks at* SANDRA, *then to* MURRAY) With a couple of years in maybe Massachusetts.

MURRAY No Massachusetts at all. Complete Bronx.

SANDRA I don't understand what . . .

MURRAY (*Sitting on the beach chair*) Oh, excuse me. Nick and I are merely testing our sense of voice and accent. Nick insists he's better at it than I am.

SANDRA (*Smiling*) As a matter of fact, the Bronx is right, but it's Grand Concourse.

MURRAY The Massachusetts thing, way off, right?

SANDRA Actually I took my graduate work with a professor, a man with a very strong New England accent, who could very well've influenced my speech. Nick is quite right.

NICK (*Proudly*) Thank you, lady.

SANDRA You certainly have a fine ear for sound, Nick. Do you and your uncle play many of these sorts of games together?

NICK Oh, yes. We play many wholesome and constructive-type games together.

MURRAY You're a big phony, Nick. Miss Markowitz has beautiful hazel eyes that have read many case histories and are ever watchful, and even clever little boys are not going to snow her. The lady is here for the facts.

ALBERT Quite so, Mr. Burns. But facts alone cannot complete our examination. (*He takes out a pen, opens to a blank page in the file*) We wish to understand . . .

NICK (*To* SANDRA, *showing off for her*) Jersey City, maybe Newark. And . . . a little bit of Chicago.

MURRAY Uh-huh. Think you've hit it, Nick.

SANDRA That's really quite remarkable. Albert—Mr. Admundson *is* from New Jersey, and he went to Chicago University for several . . .

ALBERT (*Firmly*) This is really quite beside the point, Sandra . . .

SANDRA I just think it's quite remarkable, Albert, the boy's ability to . . .

ALBERT (*Purposely interrupting her*) Suppose I just plunge right in here, before Dr. Markowitz begins her part of the interview . . .

    (*There is a noise at the front door and* ARNOLD BURNS *enters. He is carrying a medium-sized grocery delivery carton filled with a variety of fruit. He makes a rather incongruous delivery boy in that he is in his early forties and dressed in expensive, distinguished clothes, top coat, and hat. He is* MURRAY's *older brother, and his agent. It is obvious in the way he enters and automatically sets the delivery carton down on the desk that this is a daily ritual enacted at this same time every day and in this same manner.* MURRAY *does not even look up to greet him and* NICK *makes some casually mumbled greeting in his direction*)

ARNOLD The honeydew melon's in season again but not really ripe yet so . . . (*He turns, sees that there are strangers there*) Oh, sorry. Didn't know you had company . . . (*Turns, goes to the door*) See you, Nick.

NICK Yeah, see you, Uncle Arnie.
(ARNOLD *exits*)

ALBERT (*Looking at the door*) There is somebody else living here with you?

MURRAY No. That's just my brother Arnold. He brings fruit every morning on his way to the office. He's a fruit nut.

ALBERT I see here in the file that our research team spoke to your brother; your agent, I believe. We also called the people at your last business address, N.B.C. . . .

MURRAY (*Rising*) You really do a lot of that stuff, calling people, going into my personal . . .

ALBERT You've refused for quite some time, Mr. Burns, to answer any of our regular inquiries. We understand that you have been unemployed at this point for nearly five months.

NICK (*To* ALBERT) He has an excellent opportunity to be an administrative assistant . . .

ALBERT (*Pressing forward*) Other than your activities as free-lance script writer, I understand that you wrote regularly for an N.B.C. program for several years.

MURRAY I was chief writer for Leo Herman, better known as Chuckles the Chipmunk, friend of the young'uns, and seller of Chuckle-Chips, the potato chips your friend Chuckles the Chipmunk eats and chuckles over.

ALBERT And the circumstances under which you left the employ of . . .

MURRAY I quit.

ALBERT You felt that this was not the work you . . .

MURRAY I felt that I was not reaching all the boys and girls out there in Televisionland. Actually it was not so much that I wasn't reaching the boys and girls, but the boys and girls were starting to reach *me*. Six months ago, a perfectly adult bartender asked me if I wanted an onion in my martini, and I said, "Gosh n' gollies, you betcha." I knew it was time to quit.

ALBERT May I ask if this is a pattern; that is, in the past, has there been much shifting of position?

MURRAY I *always* take an onion in my martini. This is a constant and unswerving . . .

(NICK, *concerned with* MURRAY's *behavior, goes toward him in an attempt to quiet him down*)

SANDRA (*Firmly, standing*) Mr. Burns. Perhaps you are not aware of just how serious your situation is. This entire matter is a subject of intense interest to the B.C.W. The circumstances of this child's environment, the danger of . . .

ALBERT Our investigation, Mr. Burns, is the result of what the Bureau considers to be almost an emergency case.

NICK He just likes to kid around, lady. But, see, we really got a great environment here . . .

MURRAY (*To* NICK) Relax, kid. (*To* ALBERT *and* SANDRA) Look, people, I'm sorry. Let's get back to the questions.

SANDRA Fine. Nick, suppose you and I have a little chat right here.

NICK (*As he sits down next to her*) Fine. I was gonna suggest that myself.

SANDRA Nick, I bet you love to come home when you've been out playing and you get tired. You say to yourself, "Gee, I'd like to go home now."

NICK Sure. Right. And I'm happy here. Boy, if you think I'm happy now, you should see me when I'm *really* happy.

MURRAY (*To* SANDRA, *sympathetically*) He's on to you, honey. You're gonna have to be a lot foxier than that . . .

SANDRA And I'm sure that you and your uncle have a great
deal of fun together.

NICK It's not *all* laughs.

SANDRA Oh, I'm sure there are times when the fun stops and
you have nice talks and your uncle teaches you things, helps
you to . . .

NICK I can do a great Peter Lorre imitation. Murray taught
me.

ALBERT Nicky, what Miss Markowitz means, is that you and
your uncle must sometimes . . .

NICK (*In the voice of Peter Lorre, a rather good imitation*)
You can't hang me . . . I didn't do it, I tell you . . . that's
not my knife . . . I am innocent . . . it's all a mistake . . .
(MURRAY *beams, smiles proudly during imitation*)

ALBERT Nicky, that's not what we meant, we . . .

MURRAY What's the trouble? That happens to be a very good
imitation.

ALBERT Perhaps; but we are trying to . . .

MURRAY Can *you* imitate Peter Lorre?

NICK (*Confidentially, to* SANDRA) I can do a pretty good James
Cagney; I mean it's not fantastic like my Peter Lorre, but
it . . .

ALBERT (*Raising his voice a bit, somewhat commanding*)

25

Nicholas, please. Try to pay attention. Now if I may proceed to . . .

SANDRA (*Aside, to* ALBERT, *somewhat annoyed with him*) Albert, if you'll just let me handle this area. (*Then, to* NICK) Nick, let's talk about games. O.K.?

NICK O. K.

SANDRA Now, what kind of games do you like the best?

NICK Mostly I like educational games and things like that. Murray gets me to develop my natural inquiring mind.

SANDRA I wonder, do you have any favorite games or toys you'd like to show me? Some plaything that is just the most favorite one of all?

NICK I just now threw away my collection of *National Geographics* and other educational-type magazines I had a whole collection of . . .

ALBERT Nicky, Miss Markowitz is very interested in you and cares about you and everything. And if you brought out some of your favorite toys and playthings for her to see, I'm sure that she'd love them just as much as you do.

NICK Well, there's Bubbles . . .
(*He gets up to get it for them*)

MURRAY I don't think you'd be interested in seeing Bubbles . . .
(NICK *goes to a cardboard carton at the bureau, opens it,*

*and takes out a twenty-four-inch-high plastic statue of a
bare-chested hula girl. The statue is in bright colors and
has an electric switch at its pedestal.* NICK *places the
statue on the table between* ALBERT *and* SANDRA *and turns
it on*)

NICK Bubbles is what you'd call an electric statue. (*The
breasts of the statue light up and continue to blink on
and off in spectacular fashion for the next part of the scene.*
ALBERT *looks at the statue, begins busily going through the
file on his lap.* SANDRA *regards the statue scientifically, pro-
fessionally.* NICK *smiles proudly over his possession*) It's
got an electric battery timer in there that makes it go on and
off like that.

SANDRA Nick, is this your favorite toy?

NICK Well, after a while it gets pretty boring. But it's a swell
gimmick. There was another one in the store that was even
better . . .

MURRAY Anybody want orange juice or toast or anything?

SANDRA Nick, tell me . . . do you like best the fact that the
chest of the lady lights up?

NICK Well, you got to admit, you don't see boobies like that
every day. You want to see the effect when the lights are out?
When the room is dark?

SANDRA Tell me, Nick, is *that* what you like best about it, that
you can be alone in the dark with it.

NICK   Well, I don't know. But in the dark they really knock your eye out.

(ALBERT *is blinking nervously at the blinking lights of the statue*)

ALBERT   (*With strenuous calm*)   Perhaps, don't you think we ought to switch it off, turn off the . . .

SANDRA   Nick, does Bubbles, does she in any way, does her face remind you at all of, oh, let me see, your mother, for example?

NICK   (*He looks at the face of the statue*)   No. I mean, it's just a doll, it's not a statue of anybody I know. I got it in this store downtown.

SANDRA   Her chest, is that something which . . .

NICK   (*Smiling broadly*)   It's *something* all right, isn't it?

SANDRA   When you think of your mother, do you . . .

NICK   I don't think about her much.

SANDRA   But when you *do* think of her, do you remember her face best, or her *hands,* or . . .

NICK   I remember she has this terrific laugh. The kind of laugh that when she laughs it makes you laugh too. Of course, she overdoes that a lot.

SANDRA   I mean, physically, when you think of her, do you,

well, when you see Bubbles, and Bubbles goes on and off like that . . .

MURRAY Sandra, his mother's chest did not light up. Let's get that settled right now; mark it down in the file.

ALBERT (*Nervously; pointing at the blinking statue*) Nicky, I wonder if you would turn those off . . . I mean, turn *it* off, turn her off, unplug it . . .
   (MURRAY *turns the statue off, puts it back into the box*)

SANDRA Nicky, when you bought this doll . . .

MURRAY Sandy, why don't I save you a lot of time. Nick is a fairly bright kid and he knows that girls are *not* boys. Other than that his interest in ladies is confined right now to ones that light up or don't light up.

NICK I mostly like to read books that are healthy, constructive, and extremely educational for a person.

MURRAY Don't push it, Nick. He does not have any unusual fixations, Sandy. He is no more abnormally interested in your bust than Mr. Amundson is.

ALBERT Mr. Burns, it is not necessary to . . .

MURRAY Of course, I might be wrong about that.

ALBERT Our interest in that doll . . .

MURRAY You really *are* interested in that doll, Albert.

ALBERT Our interest . . .

NICK (*To* ALBERT) I'll sell it to you for two dollars. That's fifty cents less than I paid for it.
(SANDRA *is unable to suppress her amusement and laughs happily*)

ALBERT (*Quite annoyed with her*) Sandra, I fail to see . . .

SANDRA (*Controlling herself again, but still smiling*) It's just that it was funny, Albert.

ALBERT (*Taking command*) Suppose *I* pursue, then, the psychological part of . . .

SANDRA (*Bristling at him*) Excuse me, Albert, I really do feel it would be better if *I* were to . . .

MURRAY Albert, the lady was just laughing because something funny happened. That's actually the best thing to do under the circumstances.

ALBERT Mr. Burns . . .

MURRAY How would you all like to go to the Statue of Liberty? I have it on good authority from the Weather Lady that today is a beautiful day.

ALBERT Is it at all possible, Mr. Burns, for you to stick to the point?

MURRAY Albert, I bet you'd make Sandy a lot happier if you

took her off somewhere once in a while. Doesn't have to be the Statue of Liberty; actually any . . .

ALBERT My relationship with Dr. Markowitz is of no . . .

MURRAY Well, there's obviously some relationship. When Nick asked you if you'd have sugar in your coffee before, Albert, you answered for Sandy.

ALBERT Mr. Burns, this entire interview has reached a point . . .

NICK I'm going to get my educational books. I left them out on the street.
    (*He leaves the apartment, his exit unnoticed by the others*)

ALBERT This entire interview, Mr. Burns, has . . .

SANDRA Mr. Burns, I . . .

ALBERT Damn it, Sandra, don't interrupt me!

SANDRA Albert, for goodness sakes, you . . .

ALBERT (*Stands up*) Sandra, perhaps we . . . (*To* MURRAY) Would you excuse us for just a moment, Mr. Burns? I'd like to have a short conference with Sandra . . . Miss . . . Dr. Markowitz for a moment. (*She gets up.* ALBERT *and* SANDRA *walk over to the alcove, where* MURRAY *cannot hear them.* MURRAY *starts to peer at them through his binoculars until* ALBERT *turns and looks at him; he then goes to desk and tinkers with clock. Now alone with* SANDRA, ALBERT'S *manner changes somewhat. He speaks more softly and with more warmth, a departure from the stiff, professional manner he uses in dealing with* MURRAY) Sandra, what are you *doing,* have we lost all control?

SANDRA   Are you seriously talking to *me* about control?

ALBERT   Dear, I told *you* and I told Dr. Malko. It's much too soon for you to go out on cases. You need another year in the office, behind the lines, I told both of you. You're simply *not* ready.

SANDRA   Really, Albert, you hardly let me get started. I was attempting to deal with the whole child.

ALBERT   Three months out of grad school and you want to go right into the front lines. Not advisable.

SANDRA   (*Whispering angrily*)   Don't you think that this is rather stupid and unprofessional? Right here in front of him you decide to have a conference.

ALBERT   A necessity. I am supposedly the leader of our examining team . . .

SANDRA   Oh, *really* . . .

ALBERT   You get too *involved,* Sandra. Each case, you get much too emotionally involved. This is an exploratory visit, we are *scientists,* dear, you lose sight of the . . .

SANDRA   You make me sick today, Albert. This is no way to approach this man's problem. We . . .

ALBERT (*Sighing*) Oh, fine. That's just fine. Well . . . fine . . .

> (MURRAY, *at the other side of the room, picks up a megaphone*)

MURRAY (*Through the megaphone*) How are we doing? (*Puts the megaphone down, comes over to them in the alcove, sits between them; speaks sympathetically*) I personally don't feel that you're gonna work out your problems with each other. But I'm glad you came to me because I think I can help you. Al, Sandy is not going to respect you because you threaten her. Respect will have to come gradually, naturally, a maturing process . . .

ALBERT Mr. Burns . . .

MURRAY Sandy, I bet he's got a file on you.

ALBERT Mr. Burns, according to the B.C.W., the child's continuance in your home is in serious and immediate doubt. I am trying to encourage your cooperation . . . (*He is making a genuine attempt to speak warmly, understandingly*) Aren't you at all willing to answer some questions, to give some evidence in your favor for our report, some evidence to support your competency as a guardian? The Board is thoroughly aware that Nicholas is not legally adopted.

MURRAY He's my nephew. He's staying with me for a while. He's visiting.

ALBERT How long has he been here?

MURRAY Seven years.

ALBERT So you see, the Child Welfare Board has, I assure you, the right to question . . .

MURRAY (*Rises, faces* ALBERT *angrily*) You don't assure me of *any*thing, buddy, you make me damn nervous. Do you mean to tell me that four years at N.Y.U. has made you my judge? (ALBERT *shrugs, defeated; crosses to Morris chair for his coat, signals* SANDRA *that they are leaving.* MURRAY *goes toward them; speaks quietly, apologetically*) O.K., all right. What do you want to know? I'll be cooperative.
(SANDRA *and* ALBERT *sit down again*)

ALBERT Nicholas' father, where is he?

MURRAY That's not a *where* question. That's a *who* question.

ALBERT I don't quite . . .

MURRAY Nick's mother, she didn't quite either.

SANDRA She is still living . . .

MURRAY My sister is unquestionably alive.

SANDRA But her responsibility to the child.

MURRAY For five years she did everything she could for Nick . . . but get married. Now that's not easy to understand since she used to get married to *everybody*. But, somehow, having Nick matured her, she felt a responsibility not to get married to just *any*body any more, so she didn't marry Nick's father, nor was she married at the time he was born. You might call Nick a bastard, or "little bastard," depending on how whimsical you feel at the time. Is that the sort of information you wanted? . . . Ah, this situation is the social workers' paradise. What a case history, huh? . . . My sister Elaine showed up here one day with two suitcases, a hatbox, a blue parakeet, a dead gold fish, and a five-year-old child. Three days later she went downstairs to buy a pack of filter-tip cigarettes . . . (MURRAY *shrugs*) Six years later she returned for the suitcases and the hatbox . . . the parakeet I had given away, the gold fish I had long since flushed down the toilet, and the five-year-old child had, with very little effort, become six years older. When Elaine returned for her luggage I reminded her of the child and the pack of filter-tip cigarettes and suggested that this was perhaps the longest running practical joke in recent history. She was accompanied by a tall chap with sunglasses who was born to be her fifth divorce and who tried to start a small conversation with me. At this point I slapped my sister, Fifth Divorce slugged me, Sister cried, stopped quite suddenly, and then proceeded to explain to me, briefly, her well-practiced theory on the meaning of life, a philosophy falling somewhere to the left of Whoopie. At which point, I remember, I started laughing and then we all laughed and said "good-bye" like people at the end of a long party. That was almost a year ago. And I've still got Nick.

(SANDRA *is obviously sympathetic to this situation, emotionally involved in the story;* ALBERT *continues his cool professionalism, here and there jotting notes in the file*)

SANDRA But . . . but I'm sure she must have had *some* concern about Nicholas . . . about the child . . .

MURRAY His name is not Nicholas. I will admit that he has

35

stayed with that name much longer than the others . . . no, actually he was "Bill" for almost eight months . . .

SANDRA   I'm sure, on his birth certificate . . .

MURRAY   Certainly an elusive document. Not having given him a last name, Elaine felt reticent about assigning him a first one. When Nick first came here this presented a real difficulty. Nick answered to nothing whatsoever. Even the parakeet recognized its own name. Nick only knew I was calling him when he was positive there was no one else in the room.

SANDRA   (*Very much emotionally involved in this now*)   Well, how did you communicate with . . .

MURRAY   I made a deal with him when he was six, up to which time he was known rather casually as Chubby, that he could try out any name he wished, for however long he wished, until his thirteenth birthday, at which point he'd have to decide on a name he liked permanently. He went through a long period of dogs' names when he was still little, Rover and King having a real vogue there for a while. For three months he referred to himself as Big Sam, then there was Little Max, Snoopy, Chip, Rock, Rex, Mike, Marty, Lamont, Chevrolet, Wyatt, Yancy, Fred, Phil, Woodrow, Lefty, The Phantom . . . He received his library card last year in the name of Raphael Sabatini, his Cub Scout membership lists him as Barry Fitzgerald, and only last week a friend of his called asking if Toulouse could come over to his house for dinner. Nick seems to be the one that'll stick, though.

SANDRA   His mother . . . ?

MURRAY His mother, when last heard, was studying mime in Paris, having been given a sort of scholarship by a twenty-two-year-old handbag heir named Myron, who seems to believe strongly in the development of talent and student exchange. Well, I don't believe I've left anything out.

ALBERT I was not aware that Nick was an O.W. child.

MURRAY O.W.?

ALBERT Out of wedlock.

MURRAY For a moment I thought you meant Prisoner of War. I think it's that natural warmth of yours that leads me to misunderstand.

ALBERT But as concerns the child . . . (*Looks around the room*) Where *is* the child?

SANDRA You preferred not having him here anyway, Albert.

ALBERT (*Sharply*) I am perfectly aware, Sandra, of what I *prefer,* and what I do *not* prefer.

SANDRA (*Sharply*) I don't care for that tone of voice at *all,* Albert.

ALBERT (*Rises, begins to put on his coat; calmly*) Sandra, I understand perfectly what has happened. We have allowed this man to disturb us and we have *both* gotten a bit upset. Now, I really do feel that it's time we got over to that family problem in Queens. It's there in your file, the Ledbetters, the introverted child. We've really given an unreasonable amount

37

of time to this case. This interview, I'm afraid, Mr. Burns, has reached a point . . .

SANDRA (*Attempting to sound authoritative*) Albert, I personally feel that it would not be advisable to leave this particular case, at this point.

ALBERT Sandra, we have done here this morning all we . . .

SANDRA I feel that we have not really given Mr. Burns a chance to . . .

ALBERT Sandra, it's really time we left for Queens . . .

SANDRA (*Hands* ALBERT *one of her two file envelopes*) Here's the Ledbetter file, I'm staying here.

ALBERT (*Raising his voice a little*) Sandra.

SANDRA I have decided to pursue this case.

ALBERT (*Almost shouting*) Sandra, have we lost all professional control?

SANDRA (*Angry, flustered*) You just . . . you just go yourself to the Leadbellies . . . you go on to Queens.

ALBERT (*Takes her by the arm, gently, but firmly*) May I just talk to you for a moment?
(ALBERT *leads* SANDRA *over to the alcove*)

MURRAY Time out for signals again?

ALBERT (*Away from* MURRAY, *now he speaks softly, less stiffly, though still angry*) What *is* this, dear? What has happened to you today? What are you doing?

SANDRA I'm doing what I think is right.

ALBERT I know how you feel, Sandra, but there is no more we can do here.

SANDRA (*Emotionally*) I just . . . I just don't understand your behavior when you're on a case. We're supposed to be of some help, he . . .

ALBERT Of course I want to help. But don't forget that the child is the one who needs protection, who needs . . .

SANDRA Are you really going to leave that man here like that? You're not going to even try to help him or tell him what to do about the Board separating him from the child . . . I mean . . . just so cold.

ALBERT (*Takes her hand*) Dear, you spent much too much time at that graduate school and not enough time in the field. That's your whole trouble. You've got to learn your job, Sandra . . .

SANDRA (*Angry, frustrated*) Oh *really,* is that so? Albert Amundson, don't give me any of that nonsense.

ALBERT (*Glancing over at* MURRAY) Please, Sandra . . . dear, this is not the time or the place for . . .

SANDRA (*Shouting*) Graduate school wouldn't have done *you* any harm, Albert, believe *me!* Oh, this is the most terrible thing . . . (*Very close to tears*) You mean . . . you're just going to leave . . . ? Do you know what you are . . . ? you're a . . . I don't know; . . . but I'll think of something . . .

> (ALBERT *walks away, leaving her in the alcove, goes into the main room, calmly picks up his briefcase*)

ALBERT (*Retaining his control, but just a little shaken. To* MURRAY) Mr. Burns . . . You can assume at this point that Miss Markowitz is no longer involved with your case. The Board will be informed that she is no longer involved with this particular case. Her continuing here, to discuss your case . . . at this point . . . is entirely unofficial. You can dismiss any conference . . . that may resume after I leave . . . when I leave here, from your mind. And, regardless of what you think of me . . .

MURRAY I think you're a dirty O.W.

> (*Some of* SANDRA's *file papers slip from her hand and fall to the floor*)

ALBERT And . . . and do you know what *you* are? (*Readying himself to deliver a crushing insult to* MURRAY) Maladjusted! (*Goes to the door, opens it*) Good afternoon, Mr. Burns. Good afternoon, Sandra.

MURRAY Good afternoon, Mr. Amundson. Watch out crossing the street.

> (ALBERT *exits, closing door sharply behind him.* SANDRA *stands for a moment in the alcove, then begins to pick up the papers she had dropped on the floor*)

SANDRA Mr. Burns . . . (*She is making a very strong attempt to control herself, but she is obviously on the verge of tears. She goes into the main room, begins to collect her things to leave)* Mr. Burns, I must apologize to you. We . . . we have put you . . . you have been put at a disadvantage this morning. You have been involved in a personal problem that has nothing to do whatsoever with your particular case. It is entirely wrong for me to give you this impression of our . . . of our profession. *(She can no longer control herself and becomes, suddenly, a sort of child. She stands quite still, with her hands at her sides, and cries. It is not loud, hysterical crying, but intermittent and disorganized sobs, squeaks, whines, sniffles and assorted feminine noises which punctuate her speech)* Do you know what? I just lost my job. This is awful. He's right, you know. I'm not suited to my work. I get too involved. That's what he said and he's right. *(Rummaging through her purse for Kleenex)* Please don't look at me. Do you *have* to stand there? Please go away. Still, he didn't have to talk to me like that. This is the first *week* we've ever gone on cases together. I didn't think he'd behave that way. That was no way. Why don't I ever have any Kleenex? *(He gives her the closest thing at hand to blow her nose in, his undershirt from the bed.)* Thank you. *(She sits down on the bed)* Do you know that even with two fellowships it still cost me, I mean my parents mostly, it cost them seven thousand two hundred and forty-five dollars for me to go through school. I was the eighth youngest person to graduate in New York State last year and I can't stop crying. Maybe if I hurry, if I took a cab, I could still meet him in Queens.

MURRAY You can't. Queens is closed. It's closed for the season.

SANDRA Do you know what?
    (Her crying lets up a bit)

MURRAY What?

SANDRA (*With a new burst of sobs*) I hate the Ledbetters.

MURRAY Then I'm sure once I got to know them I'd hate them too.

SANDRA Mr. Burns, you don't understand. Some of the cases I love and some of them I hate, and that's all wrong for my work, but I can't help it. I hate Raymond Ledbetter and he's only nine years old and he makes me sick and I don't give a damn about him.

MURRAY (*Pointing to the file on her lap*) You can't like everybody in your portfolio.

SANDRA But some of them I like too much and worry about them all day . . . (*She is making an attempt to control her tears*) It is an obvious conflict against all professional standards. I didn't like Raymond Ledbetter so I tried to understand him, and now that I understand him I hate him.

MURRAY I think that's wonderful. Can I get you a cup of coffee?

SANDRA (*She turns to* MURRAY *as if to answer him, but instead bursts into fresh tears*) He's gone to Queens and I'll never hear from him again. I wrote out what my married name would be after dinner last night on a paper napkin, Mrs. Albert Amundson, to see how it would look. You know what I think I am, I think I'm crazy.

MURRAY Well, then, I can talk to you.

SANDRA We were going to get married. It was all planned, Mrs. Albert Amundson on a napkin. You have to understand Albert. He's really a very nice person when he's not on cases. He's a very intelligent man but last month I fell asleep twice while he was talking. I know him for so long. (*She tries once again to stop crying but the effort only increases her sobs*) Mr. Burns, don't look at me. Why don't you go away?

MURRAY But I live here.

SANDRA I would like everybody to go away.

MURRAY (*Attempting to comfort her*) Can I get you a pastrami sandwich?

SANDRA Oh, I don't know you and I'm crying right in front of you. Go away.

MURRAY Couldn't you just think of this as Show-and-Tell time?

SANDRA (*Turning away again, still seated on the bed*) The minute I got out of school I wanted to go right back inside. (*With a great sob*) Albert is gone and I just lost my job.

MURRAY (*He walks over to her*) Now, you're really going to have to stop crying, because I am going out of my mind.

SANDRA I cry all the time and I laugh in the wrong places in the movies. I am unsuited to my profession and I can't do anything right. Last night I burned an entire chicken and after seven years of school I can't work and I've got no place to go. An entire chicken.

MURRAY If I do my Peter Lorre imitation, will you stop crying?

SANDRA (*She pokes the file-envelope in her lap*) Look what I've done, I've cried on one of my files. The ink is running all over the Grumbacher twins . . .

MURRAY (*In the voice of Peter Lorre, a decent imitation*) It was all a mistake, I didn't stab Mrs. Marmalade . . . it was my knife, but someone else did it, I tell you . . .

SANDRA That's an awful imitation, Mr. Burns . . .
(*She turns away from him and sobs into the bedclothes. He takes the Bubbles statue out of the box, switches it on, places it on the floor near the bed; it starts to blink on and off. Her face peeks out, she sees the blinking statue and puts her face back into the bedclothes, but we hear some giggles mixing with her sobs now, and then overtaking them, until she finally lifts her face and we see that she is laughing*)

MURRAY (*Smiling*) There. Progress. (*He turns off the statue*) Would you like a cup of coffee, or a pastrami sandwich or something?

SANDRA No, thank you. (SANDRA *begins to compose herself, she has stopped crying completely and is wiping her eyes with the undershirt he gave her. Then she begins to fold the undershirt neatly, smoothing it out into a nice little square on her lap*) This is absolutely the most unprofessional experience I have ever had.

MURRAY People fall into two distinct categories, Miss Markowitz; people who like delicatessen, and people who don't like delicatessen. A man who is not touched by the earthy lyricism of hot pastrami, the pungent fantasy of corned beef, pickles, frankfurters, the great lusty impertinence of good mustard . . . is a man of stone and without heart. Now, Albert is obviously not a lover of delicatessen and you are well rid of him.
> (SANDRA *is still sitting on the bed, her hands folded neatly in her lap on top of her files and his undershirt*)

SANDRA What am I going to do? This is an awful day.

MURRAY (*He sits on the swivel chair next to the bed*) Miss Markowitz, this is a beautiful day and I'll tell you why. My dear, you are really a jolly old girl and you are well rid of Albert. You have been given a rare opportunity to return the unused portion and have your money refunded.

SANDRA But . . . my work . . . what am I going to . . .

MURRAY You are a lover, Dr. Markowitz, you are a lover of things and people so you took up work where you could get at as many of them as possible; and it just turned out that there were too many of them and too much that moves you. Damn it, please be glad that it turned out you are not reasonable and sensible. Have all the gratitude you can, that you are capable of embarrassment and joy and are a marathon crier.

SANDRA (*Looking directly at him*) There is a kind of relief that it's gone . . . the job, and even Albert. But I know what it is, it's just irresponsible. . . . I don't have the vaguest idea who I am. . . .

MURRAY (*He takes her hand*) It's just there's all these Sandras running around who you never met before, and it's confusing at first, fantastic, like a Chinese fire drill. But god *damn,* isn't it great to find out how many Sandras there are? Like those little cars in the circus, this tiny red car comes out and putters around, suddenly its doors open and out come a thousand clowns, whooping and hollering and raising hell.

SANDRA (*She lets go of his hand in order to pick up the undershirt in her lap*) What's this?

MURRAY That's my undershirt. How's about going to the Empire State Building with me?

SANDRA I'll have that coffee now.

MURRAY You didn't answer my question. Would you like to visit the Empire State Building?

SANDRA No, not really.

MURRAY Well, then how about the zoo?

SANDRA Not just now.

MURRAY Well, then will you marry me?

SANDRA What?

MURRAY Just a bit of shock treatment there. I have found after long experience that it's the quickest way to get a woman's attention when her mind wanders. Always works.

SANDRA Mr. Burns . . .

MURRAY Now that you've cried you can't call me Mr. Burns. Same rule applies to laughing. My name is Murray.

SANDRA Well, Murray, to sort of return to reality for a minute . . .

MURRAY I will only go as a tourist.

SANDRA Murray, you know, you're in trouble with the Child Welfare Board. They could really take Nick away. Murray, there's some things you could try to do . . . to make your case a little stronger . . .

MURRAY Sandra, do you realize that you are not wearing your shoes?

SANDRA (*She looks down at her bare feet*) Oh.
(*The front door opens and* NICK *bursts into the room, laden with books*)

NICK Well, here I am with all my favorite books, *Fun in the Rain, The Young Railroader, Great Philosophers, Science for Youth,* a Spanish dictionary. What I did was I left them out in the street when I was playing, and I went down to . . .

MURRAY Nick, you just killed a month's allowance for nothing. Miss Markowitz isn't even on our case any more.

NICK I shouldn't have left. You got angry and insulted everybody.

MURRAY Don't worry about it, Nick, we'll work it out.
(*He goes over to the closet for something*)

NICK (*Dropping his books regretfully on the chair*) Four dollars right out the window. (*To* SANDRA) Y'know, I really do read educational books and am encouraged in my home to think.

SANDRA I'm sure that's true, Nicholas, but I'm not in a position to do you much official good any more.

NICK We're in real trouble now, right? (*He turns to* MURRAY *who has taken two ukuleles from the closet and is coming toward* NICK) I figured it would happen; you got angry and hollered at everybody.

MURRAY Nick, we have a guest, a music lover. . . . (*He hands the smaller of the two ukuleles to* NICK) We've got to do our song. I am sure it will be requested.

NICK (*Protesting, gesturing with his ukulele*) Murray, stop it . . . we—this is no time to sing songs, Murray. . . .

MURRAY (*Striking a downbeat on his ukulele*) Come on, where's your professional attitude?
(MURRAY *starts playing "Yes, Sir, That's My Baby" on the ukulele, then sings the first line.* NICK *turns away at first, shaking his head solemnly at* MURRAY's *behavior.* MURRAY *goes on with the second line of the song. Reluctantly,* NICK *begins to pick out the melody on his*

48

Barry Gordon, Jason Robards, Jr., and Sandy Dennis, as
NICK BURNS, MURRAY BURNS and SANDRA MARKOWITZ

*ukulele, then he smiles in spite of himself and sings the
third line along with* MURRAY.

*They really go into the song now, singing and play-
ing "Yes, Sir, That's My Baby," doing their routine for*
SANDRA. *She sits in front of them on the bed, smiling, enjoying their act.* NICK *is in the spirit of it now and having a good time. In the middle of the song* NICK *and*
MURRAY *do some elaborate soft-shoe dance steps for a
few lines, ukuleles held aloft. This is followed by some
very fast and intricate two-part ukulele harmony on the
last few lines of the song for a big finish.*
      SANDRA *applauds.*

      MURRAY *and* NICK, *singing and strumming ukes, go
into a reprise of the song,* MURRAY *moving forward and
sitting down on the bed next to* SANDRA. NICK, *left apart
from them now, does a line or two more of the song
along with* MURRAY, *then gradually stops.* NICK *considers
them both for a moment as* MURRAY *goes on doing the
song alone now for* SANDRA. NICK *nods to himself, circles
around in front of them and, unnoticed by them, puts his
uke down on the window seat, goes to his alcove, gets
school briefcase and pajamas from his bed.* MURRAY *is
still playing the uke and singing the song to* SANDRA *as*
NICK *goes past them on his way to the front door, carrying his stuff)*

NICK (*Pleasantly, to* SANDRA) Nice to meet you, lady. I'll see
you around.

MURRAY (*Stops singing, turns to* NICK) Where you off to,
Nick?

NICK Gonna leave my stuff up at Mrs. Myers'. (*Opens the door*) I figure I'll be staying over there tonight.

(NICK *exits, waving a pleasant good-bye to* SANDRA. SANDRA *looks at the front door, puzzled; then she looks at* MURRAY, *who resumes the song, singing and strumming the uke*)

Curtain

ACT TWO

ACT TWO

Scene: MURRAY'S *apartment, eight* A.M. *the following morning.*

At rise: The phone is ringing loudly on the window seat.
MURRAY *enters from the bathroom with his toothbrush in his
mouth, grabs the phone. The room is as it was at the end of
Act One except that there is a six-foot-high folding screen
placed around the bed, hiding it from view, and the shades
are drawn again on the windows.*

MURRAY (*Speaks immediately into the phone*) Is this somebody with good news or money? No? Good-bye. (*He hangs
up*) It's always voices like that you hear at eight A.M. Mani-
acs. (*He pulls up the shade to see what kind of a day it is
outside. As usual the lighting of the room changes not at all
with the shade up, as before he sees nothing but the blank,
grayish wall opposite*) Crap. (*With a sigh of resignation,
he picks up the phone, dials, listens*) Hello, Weather Lady.
I am fine, how are you? What is the weather? Uh-huh . . .
uh-huh . . . uh-huh . . . very nice. Only a *chance* of
showers? Well, what exactly does that . . . Aw, there she
goes again . . . (*He hangs up*) Chance of showers. (*The
phone rings. He picks it up, speaks immediately into it*)
United States Weather Bureau forecast for New York City
and vicinity: eight A.M. temperature, sixty-five degrees, somewhat cooler in the suburbs, cloudy later today with a
chance of . . . (*Looks incredulously at the phone*) He
hung up. Fool. Probably the most informative phone call
he'll make all day. (*He stands, opens the window, leans out,
raising his voice, shouting out the window*) This is your
neighbor speaking! Something must be done about your

53

garbage cans in the alley here. It is definitely second-rate
garbage! By next week I want to see a better class of garbage,
more empty champagne bottles and caviar cans! So let's *snap*
it up and get on the *ball!*

(SANDRA's *head appears at the top of the screen, like a
puppet's head. She is staring blankly at* MURRAY. MURRAY
*steps toward her, she continues to stare blankly at him.
Her head suddenly disappears again behind the screen.
The screen masks the entire bed and* SANDRA *from his
view, and the view of audience. We hear a rustle of
sheets and blankets, silence for a couple of seconds, and
then* SANDRA's *voice; she speaks in a cold, dignified, lady-
like voice, only slightly tinged with sleep, impersonal,
polite, and distant, like one unintroduced party guest to
another)*

SANDRA   Good morning.

MURRAY   Good morning.

SANDRA   How are you this morning?

MURRAY   I am fine this morning. How are you?

SANDRA   I am fine also. Do you have a bathrobe?

MURRAY   Yes, I have a bathrobe.

SANDRA   May I have your bathrobe, please?

MURRAY   I'll give you Nick's. It'll fit you better.

SANDRA   That seems like a good idea.

(He takes NICK's *bathrobe from the hook in the alcove, tosses it over the top of the screen)*

MURRAY   There you go.

SANDRA   *(Her voice from behind the screen is getting even colder)*   Thank you. What time is it?

MURRAY   It is eight-fifteen and there is a chance of showers. Did you sleep well?

SANDRA   Yes. How long have you been up?

MURRAY   Little while.

SANDRA   Why didn't you wake me?

MURRAY   Because you were smiling. *(Silence for a moment)* How does the bathrobe fit?

SANDRA   This bathrobe fits fine. *(After a moment)*   Did you happen to see my clothes?

MURRAY   *(Starts for the bathroom)*   They're in the bathroom. Shall I get them?

SANDRA   No, thank you. *(She suddenly pops out from behind the screen and races across the room into the kitchen at right, slamming the kitchen door behind her. We hear her voice from behind the door)*   This isn't the bathroom. This is the kitchen.

MURRAY   If it *was* the bathroom then this would be a very extreme version of an efficiency apartment. (*He goes to the bathroom to get her clothes, brings them with him to the kitchen door. He knocks on the door*) Here are your clothes. Also toothpaste and toothbrush.

(*The kitchen door opens slightly, her hand comes out. He puts the stuff in it, her hand goes back, the door closes again*)

SANDRA Thank you.

MURRAY Sandy, is everything all right?

SANDRA What?

MURRAY I said, is everything all right?

SANDRA Yes. I'm using the last of your toothpaste.

MURRAY That's all right. There's soap by the sink.

SANDRA I know. I found it.

MURRAY That's good.

SANDRA It was right by the sink.

MURRAY Suppose we broaden this discussion to other matters . . .

SANDRA I saw the soap when I came in.
(*The front door opens and* ARNOLD BURNS *enters as he did before, carrying a grocery carton filled with varieties of fruit. He sets it down on the desk*)

ARNOLD Morning, Murray.

MURRAY (*Without turning to look at him*) Morning, Arnold.

ARNOLD Murray, Chuckles called again yesterday. I told him I'd talk to you. And Jimmy Sloan is in from the coast; he's putting a new panel-show package together . . .

MURRAY Arnold, you have many successful clients . . .

ARNOLD Murray . . .

MURRAY With all these successful people around, where are all of our new young failures going to come from?

ARNOLD Murray, those people I saw here yesterday; they were from the Welfare Board, right? I tried to warn you . . .

MURRAY Nothing to worry about.

ARNOLD These Welfare people don't kid around.

MURRAY Arnold, I don't mind you coming with fruit if you keep quiet, but you bring a word with every apple . . . Everything's fine. You'll be late for the office.

ARNOLD Is Nick all right?

MURRAY Fine.

ARNOLD O.K., good-bye, Murray.

MURRAY Good-bye, Arnold. (ARNOLD *exits*. MURRAY *talks to the*

57

closed kitchen door again) There's coffee still in the pot from last night, if you want to heat it up.

SANDRA   I already lit the flame.

MURRAY   Good. The cups are right over the sink. Will you be coming out soon?

SANDRA   I found the cups.

MURRAY   Do you think you will be coming out soon?

SANDRA   Yes, I think so. Cream and sugar in your coffee?

MURRAY   Yes, thank you.

SANDRA   Murray.

MURRAY   Yes.

SANDRA   I'm coming out now.

MURRAY   That's good.

SANDRA   I'm all finished in here so I'm coming out now.

MURRAY   That's very good.
  (*The kitchen door opens.* SANDRA, *dressed neatly, comes out of the kitchen, carrying two cups of coffee and* NICK's *bathrobe*)

SANDRA   (*Pausing at kitchen doorway, smiles politely*)   Well, here I am. (*She goes to* MURRAY, *gives him a cup, sits on swivel chair. He sits next to her, on the stool. She takes a sip of coffee, straightens her hair. She is quite reserved, though pleasant; she behaves as though at a tea social)* You know, yesterday was the first time I've ever been to the Statue of Liberty. It's funny how you can live in a city for so long and not visit one of its most fascinating sights.

MURRAY That is funny. (*He sips his coffee*) This coffee isn't bad, for yesterday's coffee.

SANDRA I think it's very good, for yesterday's coffee. (*Takes another sip*) What kind of coffee is it?

MURRAY I believe it's Chase and Sanborn coffee.

SANDRA "Good to the last drop," isn't that what they say?

MURRAY I think that's Maxwell House.

SANDRA Oh yes. Maxwell House coffee. "Good to the last drop."

MURRAY It's Chase and Sanborn that used to have the ad about the ingredients: "Monizalles for mellowness" was one.

SANDRA They used to sponsor Edgar Bergen and Charlie McCarthy on the radio.

MURRAY Yes. You're right.

SANDRA "Monizalles for mellowness." I remember. That's right. (*She finishes her coffee, puts her cup down on the table. Then, after a moment*) I have to leave now.

59

MURRAY Oh?

SANDRA Yes. I'll have to be on my way.
(She stands, takes her pocketbook, puts on her shoes and starts to exit)

MURRAY *(Takes her files from the floor, hands them to her)* Don't forget your files.

SANDRA Oh yes. My files. *(She takes them from him, stands looking at him)* Well, good-bye.

MURRAY Good-bye, Sandra.

SANDRA Good-bye.
(She walks out of the apartment, and closes the door behind her. Alone in the apartment now, MURRAY stands for a moment looking at the door. He then runs to open the door; she has had her hand on the outside knob and is dragged into the room as he does so)

MURRAY *(Laughing, relieved)* You nut. I was ready to kill you.

SANDRA *(Throws her arms around him, drops her bag and files on floor)* What happened? You didn't say anything. I was waiting for you to say something. Why didn't you say something or kiss me or . . .

MURRAY I was waiting for *you*, for God's sake.
(He kisses her)

SANDRA I didn't know *what* was going on. *(She kisses him, their arms around each other; he leans away from her for a moment to put his coffee cup on the table)* Don't let me go . . .

MURRAY   I was just putting my coffee cup down . . .

SANDRA   Don't let me go. (*He holds her tightly again*)   Murray, I thought about it, and I probably love you.

MURRAY   That's very romantic. I probably love you too. You have very small feet. For a minute yesterday, it looked like you only had four toes, and I thought you were a freak. I woke up in the middle of the night and counted them. There are five.

SANDRA   I could have told you that.

MURRAY   (*He sits in the swivel chair; she is on his lap*)   You knocked down maybe seven boxes of Crackerjacks yesterday. You are twelve years old. You sleep with the blanket under your chin like a napkin. When you started to talk about the coffee before, I was going to throw you out the window except there'd be no place for you to land but the trash can from the Chinese restaurant.

SANDRA   You mean that you live above a Chinese restaurant?

MURRAY   Yes. It's been closed for months, though.

SANDRA   Do you mean that you live above an abandoned Chinese restaurant?

MURRAY   Yes, I do.

SANDRA That's wonderful. (*She kisses him; jumps up from his lap happily excited about what she has to say. Takes off her jacket and hangs it on the back of the Morris chair*) I didn't go to work this morning and I simply can't tell you how fantastic that makes me feel. I'm not going to do a *lot* of things any more. (*Picks at the material of her blouse*) This blouse I'm wearing, my mother picked it out, everybody picks out things for me. She gets all her clothes directly from Louisa May Alcott. (*Picks up the stool, changes its position in the room*) Well, we've all seen the last of this blouse anyway. Do you realize that I feel more at home here after twenty-four hours than I do in my parents' house after twenty-five years? Of course, we'll have to do something about curtains . . . and I hope you didn't mind about the screen around the bed, I just think it gives such a nice, separate bedroomy effect to that part of the room . . . (*Picks up her bag and files from the floor where she dropped them, puts them in the closet. She is moving in*) Oh, there are so many wonderful tricks you can try with a one-room apartment, really, if you're willing to use your imagination . . . (*He watches helplessly as she moves happily about the apartment judging it with a decorator's eye*) I don't care if it sounds silly, Murray, but I was projecting a personality identification with the Statue of Liberty yesterday . . . courageous and free and solid metal . . . (*She kisses him, then continues pacing happily*) I was here with you last night and I don't give a damn who knows it or what anybody thinks, and that goes for Dr. Malko, Albert, my mother, Aunt Blanche . . . Oh, I'm going to do so many things I've always wanted to do.

MURRAY For example.

SANDRA Well . . . I'm not sure right now. And that's marvel-
ous too, I am thoroughly enjoying the idea that I don't know
what I'm going to do next. (*Stops pacing*) Do you have an
extra key?

MURRAY What?

SANDRA An extra key. Altman's has this terrific curtain sale,
thought I'd go and . . .

MURRAY Well, then I'd better give you some money . . .

SANDRA No, that's all right. (*Holds out her hand*) Just the
key.

MURRAY Oh.
   (*He looks at her blankly for a moment, then reaches into
   his pocket slowly, finds the key, slowly hands it to her*)

SANDRA (*Snatches up the key, goes on delightedly pacing up
and down*) Murray, did we bring back any Crackerjacks?

MURRAY (*Pointing to some packages on the desk*) Only stuff
we brought back was that cleaning equipment. I'll admit this
place is a little dirty, but all that stuff just for . . .
   (*The doorbell rings.* SANDRA *flinches for a moment, but
   then smiles and stands firmly*)

SANDRA You'd better answer it, Murray.

MURRAY Sandra, would you prefer to . . .

(He indicates the kitchen as a hiding place, but she stands right where she is, refusing to move)

SANDRA   I've got no reason to hide from anybody.
   (MURRAY goes to the front door and opens it halfway, but enough for us to see the visitor, ALBERT AMUNDSON. ALBERT cannot see beyond the door to where SANDRA is standing)

ALBERT   Good morning, Mr. Burns.

MURRAY   Albert, how are you?
   (SANDRA, hearing ALBERT's voice, and realizing who it is, goes immediately into the closet, closing the door behind her)

ALBERT   May I come in?

MURRAY   Sure.
   (MURRAY opens the front door all the way, allowing ALBERT into the main room. MURRAY closes the door, then follows ALBERT into the room. MURRAY smiles to himself when he sees that SANDRA is not there and then glances at the closet door)

ALBERT   I called you twice this morning, Mr. Burns.

MURRAY   That was you.

ALBERT   That was me. Miss Markowitz did not show up in Queens yesterday.

MURRAY   So?

ALBERT Her parents are quite upset. I am quite upset. Where is she?

MURRAY She's hiding in the closet.

ALBERT We're really all quite anxious to know where she is.

MURRAY I'm not kidding. She's in the closet.
(ALBERT *goes to the closet, opens the door, sees* SANDRA, *then closes the door.* ALBERT *comes back to* MURRAY)

ALBERT She *is* in the closet.

MURRAY I wouldn't lie to you, Albert.

ALBERT Why is she in the closet?

MURRAY I don't know. She's got this thing about closets.

ALBERT That's a very silly thing for her to be in that closet.

MURRAY Don't knock it till you've tried it. Now, what else can I do for you?

ALBERT That's a difficult thing for me to believe. I mean, that she's right there in the closet. You are not a person, Mr. Burns, you are an experience.

MURRAY (*Goes into the kitchen*) That's very nice, Albert, I'll have to remember that.

ALBERT Actually, Dr. Markowitz is not the reason for my visit today. I came here in an official capacity.

MURRAY (*From the kitchen*) You don't wear an official capacity well, Albert. Coffee?

ALBERT No, thank you.
(MURRAY *brings the pot out, fills the two cups on the table; brings one of the cups of coffee to the closet and hands it through the partly open door*)

MURRAY (*Returns to the table, sits opposite* ALBERT) What have you got on your mind, Albert?

ALBERT (*Sits; begins hesitantly*) Burns, late yesterday afternoon the Child Welfare Board made a decision on your case. Their decision is based on three months of a thorough study; our interview yesterday is only a small part of the . . . I want you to understand that I am not responsible, personally, for the decision they've reached, I . . .

MURRAY Relax, Albert, I won't even hold you responsible for the shadow you're throwing on my rug.

ALBERT For eleven months you have avoided contact with the Board, made a farce of their inquiries. You are not employed, show no inclination to gain employment, have absolutely no financial stability . . .

MURRAY Look, Albert, I . . .

ALBERT Months of research by the Board and reports by the Revere School show a severe domestic instability, a libertine self-indulgence, a whole range of circumstances severely detrimental to the child's welfare . . .

66

MURRAY Look, stop the tap-dancing for a second, Albert; what's going on, what . . .

ALBERT It is the Board's decision that you are unfit to be the guardian of your nephew, and that action be taken this Friday to remove the child from this home and the deprivation you cause him.

MURRAY You mean they can really . . . (*Sips his coffee, putting on an elaborate display of calm, showing no emotion*) Where'd they get this routine from, Charles Dickens?

ALBERT The Board is prepared to find a more stable, permanent home for your nephew, a family with whom he will live a more wholesome, normal . . .

MURRAY Look, Albert, there must be some kind of a hearing or something, where I'll have a chance to . . .

ALBERT You will have the opportunity Thursday to state your case to the Board. If there is some substantial change in your circumstances, some evidence they're not aware of; if you can demonstrate that you are a responsible member of society . . .

MURRAY It's Tuesday; what the hell am I supposed to do in two days, win the Nobel Peace Prize? They sent you here to tell me this?

ALBERT No, you were to be informed by the court. But in view of the confusion which took place here yesterday, for which I consider myself responsible, I felt it my duty to come here and explain . . .

MURRAY Buddy, you speak like you write everything down before you say it.

ALBERT Yes, I do speak that way, Mr. Burns. I wish that I spoke more spontaneously. I realize that I lack warmth. I will always appear foolish in a conversation with a person of your imagination. Please understand, there is no vengeance in my activities here. I love my work, Mr. Burns. I believe that you are a danger to this child. I wish this were not true, because it is obvious that you have considerable affection for your nephew. It is in your face, this feeling. I admire you for your warmth, Mr. Burns, and for the affection the child feels for you. I admire this because I am one for whom children do not easily feel affection. I am not one of the warm people. But your feeling for the child does not mollify the genuinely dangerous emotional climate you have made for him. (*He moves toward* MURRAY) I wish you could understand this, I would so much rather you understood, could really hear what I have to say. For yours is, I believe, a distorted picture of this world.

MURRAY Then why don't you send *me* to a foster home?

ALBERT I was right. You really can't listen to me. You are so sure of your sight. Your villains and heroes are all so terribly clear to you, and I am obviously one of the villains. (*Picks up his briefcase*) God save you from your vision, Mr. Burns. (*Goes to the front door, opens it*) Good-bye.
  (ALBERT *exits*)

MURRAY (*Stands at the window with his coffee cup in his hand, looking out at gray, blank wall of the building opposite*) Hey, courageous, free one, you can come out now.

(SANDRA *comes out of closet carrying her coffee cup;*
MURRAY *does not look at her*)

SANDRA I'm sorry, Murray. I'm really very embarrassed. I don't
know what happened. I just ran into the closet. And . . .
and once I was in there, I just didn't want to come out. I'm
sorry, Murray . . .

MURRAY Don't be nervous, lady, you're just going through an
awkward stage. You're between closets. (*Quietly, calmly*)
Look, if Nick has to leave, if he goes, he goes, and my life
stays about the same. But it's no good for *him,* see, not for a
couple of years, anyway. Right now he's still ashamed of
being sharper than everybody else, he could easily turn into
another peeled and boiled potato. Are you listening to me?

SANDRA Yes, of course . . .

MURRAY Well, make some kind of listening noise then, will
you? Wink or nod your head or something.

SANDRA But, I'm . . .

MURRAY (*Casually; gesturing with his coffee cup*) Tell you
the truth, it's even a little better for me if he goes. I mean,
he's a middle-aged kid. When I signed with the network he
sat up all night figuring out the fringe benefits and the pen-
sion plan. And he started to make *lists* this year. Lists of
everything; subway stops, underwear, what he's gonna do
next week. If somebody doesn't watch out he'll start making
lists of what he's gonna do next year and the next ten years.
Hey, suppose they put him in with a whole family of list-
makers? (*Angrily*) I didn't spend six years with him so he

69

should turn into a listmaker. He'll learn to know everything before it happens, he'll learn to plan, he'll learn how to be one of the nice dead people. Are you listening?

SANDRA Of course, I told you, Murray, I . . .

MURRAY Then stamp your feet or mutter so I'll know you're there, huh? (*Still speaking quite calmly*) I just want him to stay with me till I can be sure he won't turn into Norman Nothing. I want to be sure he'll know when he's chickening out on himself. I want him to get to know exactly the special thing he is or else he won't notice it when it starts to go. I want him to stay awake and know who the phonies are, I want him to know how to holler and put up an argument, I want a little guts to show before I can let him go. I want to be sure he sees all the wild possibilities. I want him to know it's worth all the trouble just to give the world a little goosing when you get the chance. And I want him to know the subtle, sneaky, important reason why he was born a human being and not a chair. (*Pause*) I will be very sorry to see him go. That kid was the best straight man I ever had. He is a laugher, and laughers are rare. I mean, you tell that kid something funny . . . not just any piece of corn, but something funny, and he'll give you your money's worth. It's not just funny jokes he reads, or I tell him, that he laughs at. Not just set-up funny stuff. He sees street jokes, he has the good eye, he sees subway farce and crosstown-bus humor and all the cartoons that people make by being alive. He has a good eye. And I don't want him to leave until I'm certain he'll never be ashamed of it. (*Still quite calmly, unemotionally*) And in addition to that . . . besides that . . . see (*Suddenly; loudly*) Sandy, I don't want him to go. I like having him around here. What should I do, Sandy? Help me out. (*Suddenly slumps forward in his chair, covers his face with his hands; very quietly*) I like when he reads me from the want ads.

SANDRA (*Takes his hands*) Murray, don't worry, we'll do something. I know the Board, their procedure, there's things you can do . . .

MURRAY (*Quietly, thoughtfully*) What I'll do is I'll buy a new suit. The first thing is to get a dignified suit.

SANDRA If you could get some kind of a job, get your brother to help you.

MURRAY Right. Right.

SANDRA Is there something you can get in a hurry?

MURRAY Sure, one of those summer suits with the ready-made cuffs . . .

SANDRA No, I mean a job. If we could just bring some proof of employment to the hearing, Murray, show them how anxious you are to change. We'll show them you want to be reliable.

MURRAY (*Brightening*) Yeah, reliable . . . (*Rises; going toward the phone*) Sandy, we will put on a God-damned show for them. Spectacular reliability; a reliability parade; bands, floats, everything. (*Starts to dial*) Sandy, go to the files and pick me out a tie that is quiet but at the same time projects a mood of inner strength. (*Into the phone*) Arnold Burn's office, please.

71

SANDRA (*On her way to the file cabinet*) One quiet tie with a mood of inner strength.

MURRAY (*Into the phone*) Hello, Margot? It's Murray. Oh, well, when Arnie comes in here's what you do. First you tell him to sit down. Then you tell him I want to get a job. When he has recovered sufficiently from that shock, tell him . . . (SANDRA *comes to him with a tie*) Excuse me a second, Margot . . . (*To* SANDRA, *indicating the tie*) Yes, quiet but with strength. (SANDRA *laughs*) Sandy, that is the greatest happy laugh I ever heard on a lady. Do that again. (*She laughs again*) Great. Keep that laugh. I'll need it later. (*Into the phone*) Margot, tell him I'm going downtown to pick up a new suit for myself and a beautiful pineapple for him, call him back in about an hour, O.K.? Thanks, Margot.
(*Puts the phone down, goes to get his jacket*)

SANDRA Can I come with you? I'd love to buy a suit with you.

MURRAY (*Putting on his jacket*) Better not, Sandy. Gotta move fast. These shoes look O.K.? (*She nods, he takes her hand*) Look, don't go away.

SANDRA I won't.
(*She kisses him*)

MURRAY (*Goes to the front door; turns to her, smiles*) Say "Good luck."

SANDRA Good luck.

MURRAY (*Opening the door*) Now say "You are a magnificent human being."

SANDRA You are a magnificent human being.

MURRAY (*As he exits*) I *thought* you'd notice.
(*She stands in door and watches him go as the lights
fade out quickly. Immediately, as the lights fade, we
hear the voice of Chuckles the Chipmunk* (LEO HERMAN)

LEO'S VOICE Hi there, kidderoonies; there's nothin' more lone-
lier than a lonely, little looney Chippermunk. So won't ya
please come on along with me fer a fun hour, 'cuz that lone-
liest, littlest, looniest Chippermunk, is *me* . . . Chuckles.
(*Lights come up now in* ARNOLD BURNS' *office, later that
afternoon. The office is part of a large theatrical agency of
which* ARNOLD *is a rather successful member; modern, wood-
paneling, nonobjective paintings and framed photographs of
his clients on the wall, a spectacularly large window behind
the desk with a twenty-second-floor skyline view. A large
bowl of fruit is on an end table near the door. One of the
two phones on* ARNOLD's *desk is a special speaker-phone, con-
sisting of a small loudspeaker box on the desk which ampli-
fies clearly the voice of whoever is calling. It can also be
spoken into from almost any point in the room if one is facing it. As the following scene progresses the speaker-phone
is treated by those present as if it were a person in the room,
they gesture to it, smile at it.* ARNOLD *is alone in his office,
leaning against his desk, listening to the speaker-phone, from
which we continue to hear the voice of* LEO HERMAN) God
damn it, Arn; that's the intro Murray wrote for me two
years ago, and it's still lovely, still warm. It's the way the kids
know me, the way I say "Hello, kids"; he's a sweetie of a
writer.

ARNOLD That was *last* year he won the sweetie award, Leo.

73

LEO's VOICE (*Laughs good-naturedly*) Please excuse my little words. They slip out of my face once in a while. Arn, you got my voice comin' out of that speaker-phone in your office, huh? Comes out like the biggest phony you ever met, right? That's how I sound, don't I? Big phony.

ARNOLD No, Leo.

LEO's VOICE I'm getting sick of myself. Hey, Arn, you figure there's a good chance of Murray comin' back with me on the show?

ARNOLD Can't guarantee it, Leo; I've sent him to one other appointment today, fairly good offer . . .

LEO's VOICE Well, I'm hopin' he comes back with *me*, Arn. Funny bit you being the agent for your own brother—what d'ya call that?

ARNOLD It's called incest. (*The intercom buzzes;* ARNOLD *picks it up*) O.K., send him in. (*Into the speaker-phone*) Got a call, fellah; check back with you when Murray shows.

LEO's VOICE Right, 'bye now.
> (MURRAY *enters wearing a new suit and carrying a beautiful pineapple*)

MURRAY Good afternoon, Mr. Burns.

ARNOLD Good afternoon, Mr. Burns. Hey, you really did get a new suit, didn't you? How'd the appointment go with . . .

MURRAY (*Putting the pineapple on the desk, gestures around at the office*) Arnold, every time I see you, the agency's put you on a higher floor. I swear, next time I come you'll be up in a balloon.

ARNOLD Murray, the appointment . . .

MURRAY Can't get over this office, Arnie. (*Goes to the window, looks out*) Twenty-second floor. You can see everything. (*Shocked by something he sees out of the window*) My God, I don't believe it: it's King Kong. He's sitting on top of the Time-Life Building. He . . . he seems to be crying. Poor gorilla bastard, they shoulda told him they don't make those buildings the way they used to . . .

ARNOLD (*Raising his hand in the air*) Hello, Murray, hello there . . . here we are in my office. Welcome to Tuesday. Now, come *on,* how'd it go with Jimmy Sloan?

MURRAY He took me to lunch at Steffanos, East Fifty-third. Christ, it's been a coupla years since I hustled around lunchland. There is this crazy hum that I haven't heard for so long, Arnie; eight square yards of idea men, busily having ideas, eating away at their chef's salad like it's Crackerjacks and there's a prize at the bottom.

ARNOLD And Sloan . . . ?

MURRAY (*Sitting on the sofa*) Sloan lunches beautifully, can out-lunch anybody. He used to be a Yes-man but he got himself some guts and now he goes around bravely saying "maybe" to everybody. And a killer, this one, Arnie; notches on his attaché case. Told me this idea he had where I'd be a lovable eccentric on his panel show. This somehow led him very logically to his conception of God, who he says is "probably a really fun guy."

ARNOLD What'd you tell him about the offer?

MURRAY I told him good-bye. I don't think he noticed when I left; he focuses slightly to the right of you when he talks, just over your shoulder, so if you stay out of range he can't tell that you're gone. Probably thinks I'm still there.

ARNOLD Murray, you told me this morning to get any job I could; Sloan's offer wasn't so bad . . .

MURRAY Sloan is an idiot.

ARNOLD (*Sitting next to him on the sofa; angrily, firmly*) Listen, cookie, I got *news* for you, right now you *need* idiots. You got a bad reputation for quitting jobs; I even had trouble grabbing Sloan for you. Why did you have to go and build your own personal blacklist; why couldn't you just be blacklisted as a Communist like everybody else?

MURRAY Don't worry, Arnie; I figured I'd go back with Chuckles. He's ready to take me back, isn't he?

ARNOLD Yeah, he's ready. I just spoke to him. (*Solemnly*) Hey, Murray, Leo says he came up to your place last January, a week after you quit him, to talk you into coming back with the show. And right in the middle you went into the kitchen and started singing "Yes, Sir, That's My Baby." Just left him standing there. Your way of saying "good-bye."

MURRAY Well, that was five months ago, Arnie . . .

ARNOLD (*Attempts to conceal his amusement, then turns to* MURRAY, *smiling*) So, what'd you do with him, just left him standing there? (*He laughs*) Like to have been there, seen that, must have been great.

MURRAY Arnie, it was beautiful.

ARNOLD (*Still laughing*) It's about time somebody left Leo Herman standing around talking to himself. (*Rubbing his head*) I wish to God I didn't enjoy you so much. Crap, I don't do you any good at all. (*Then, solemnly again*) Murray, no fun and games with Leo today, understand? He is absolutely *all* we got left before the hearing Thursday.

MURRAY Yes, I understand.

ARNOLD (*Goes to pick up the phone on the desk*) I wish we coulda got something better for you, kid, but there just wasn't any time.

MURRAY Well, Chuckles won't be so bad for a while . . .

ARNOLD No, Murray. (*Puts phone down firmly*) Not just for a while. You'll really have to stick with Chuckles. I had our agency lawyer check the facts for me. Most the Board'll give you is a probationary year with Nick; a trial period. The Board's investigators will be checking on you every week . . .

MURRAY That's charming.

ARNOLD . . . checking to see if you've still got the job, checking with Leo on your stability, checking up on the change in your home environment.

MURRAY Sounds like a parole board.

ARNOLD (*Into the intercom phone*) Margot; get me Leo Herman on the speaker-phone here, his home number. Thanks. (*Puts the phone down*) He's waiting for our call. Look, Murray, maybe he's not the greatest guy in the world; but y'know, he really *likes* you, Murray, he . . .

MURRAY Yeah. I have a way with animals.

ARNOLD (*Pointing at* MURRAY) That was your last joke for today. (*A click is heard from speaker-phone;* ARNOLD *turns it on*) You there, Leo?

LEO's VOICE Right, Arn. I'm down here in the basement, in my gymnasium; lot of echoing. Am I coming through, am I coming through O.K.?

ARNOLD Clearly, Leo. Murray's here.

LEO's VOICE Murray! Murray the wonderful wild man; fellah, how are ya?

MURRAY (*Takes his hat off, waves hello to the speaker-phone*) O.K., Leo, how're you doing?

LEO's VOICE Oh, you crazy bastard, it's damn good to hear that voice again. You're an old monkey, aren't ya?

MURRAY You sound about the same too, Leo.

LEO's VOICE Not the same. I'm *more impossible* than I used to be. Can you imagine that?

MURRAY   Not easily, Leo; no.

LEO'S VOICE   Murray, I need you, fellah; I need you back with the show. Murr', we'll talk a while now, and then I'll come over to your place tonight, go over some ideas for next week's shows. It'll be great, sweetie . . . Oh, there's that word again. "Sweetie." I said that word again. Oh, am I getting *sick* of myself. Big phony. The truth, fellah, I'm the biggest phony you ever met, right?

MURRAY   Probably, Leo.

LEO'S VOICE   (*After a pause; coldly*)   Probably, he says. There he goes, there goes Murray the old joker, right? You're a jester, right? Some fooler. You can't fool with a scheduled show, Murray; a scheduled show with a tight budget. (*Softly, whispering*)   Murray, come closer, tell you a secret . . . (MURRAY *comes closer to the box*)   You're gonna hate me, Murray; I gotta tell you something and I know you're gonna hate me for it, but we can't have the same Murray we used to have on the show. Who appreciates a good joke more than anybody? *Me.* But who jokes too much? (*Suddenly louder*) *You!*

MURRAY   Leo, couldn't we talk about this tonight when we get together . . .

LEO'S VOICE   (*Softly again*)   It hurt me, Murr', it hurt me what you used to do. When all those thousands of kids wrote in asking for the definition of a chipmunk and you sent back that form letter sayin' a chipmunk was a . . . was a what?

MURRAY   A cute rat.

79

LEO's VOICE (*Still soft*) A cute rat; yeah. I remember my skin broke out somethin' terrible. Some jester you are, foolin' around at the script conferences, foolin' around at the studio. Now, we're not gonna have any more of that, are we?

MURRAY (*Subservient, apologetic*) No, we won't, I'm sorry, Leo.

LEO's VOICE Because we can't fool with the innocence of children, can we? My God, they believe in the little Chipmunk, don't ask me why; I'm nothing; God, I know that. I've been damned lucky. A person like me should get a grand and a half a week for doin' nothin'. I mean, I'm one of the big no-talents of all time, right?

MURRAY Right . . . I mean, no, Leo, no.

LEO's VOICE Oh, I know it's the truth and I don't kid myself about it. But there'll be no more jokin'; right, Murr'? Because I'll tell you the truth, I can't stand it.

MURRAY Right, Leo.

LEO's VOICE (*Softly*) Good. Glad we cleared that up. Because my skin breaks out somethin' terrible. (*Up again*) You're the best, Murray, such talent, you know I love ya, don't ya? You old monkey.

MURRAY (*To* ARNOLD) Please, tell him we'll talk further to-night, too much of him all at once . . .

ARNOLD Say, Leo, suppose we . . .

LEO'S VOICE Murray, I want you to put some fifteen-minute fairy tales into the show. You've got your Hans Christian Andersen's there, your Grimm Brothers, your Goldilocks, your Sleepin' Beauties, your Gingerbread Men, your Foxy-Loxies, your legends, your folk tales . . . do I reach ya, Murr'?

MURRAY (*Quietly*) Yeah, Leo . . .

LEO'S VOICE Now, what I want in those scripts is this, Murray, I want you to give 'em five minutes a action, five minutes a poignancy and then five minutes of the moral message; race-relations thing; world-peace thing; understanding-brings-love thing. I don't know. Shake 'em up a little. Controversy. Angry letters from parents. Kid's show with something to say, get some excitement in the industry, wild . . .

MURRAY (*He leans over very close to speaker-phone; whispers into it*) Hey, Leo, I might show up one day with eleven minutes of poignancy, no action and a twelve-second moral message . . .

ARNOLD Murray, stop it . . .

MURRAY (*Shouting into the speaker-phone*) *And then where would we be?*
(*There is a pause. No sound comes from the speaker-phone. Then:*)

LEO'S VOICE See how he mocks me? Well, I guess there's plenty to mock. Plenty mocking. Sometimes I try to take a cold look at what I am. (*Very soft*) Sweaty Leo jumping around in a funny costume trying to make a buck out of

81

being a chipmunk. The Abominable Snowman in a cute suit. But I'll tell you something, Murray . . . sit down for a minute. (MURRAY *is standing;* LEO's VOICE *is still fairly pleasant*) Are ya sitting down, Murray? (MURRAY *remains standing;* LEO's VOICE *is suddenly loud, sharp, commanding*) Murray, sit down! (MURRAY *sits down*) Good. Now I'm gonna tell you a story . . .

MURRAY (*Softly, painfully*) Arnold, he's gonna do it again . . . the story . . .

LEO's VOICE Murray . . .

MURRAY (*Softly, miserably*) The story I got tattooed to my skull . . .

LEO's VOICE On June the third . . .

MURRAY (*Hunching over in his chair, looking down at the floor*) Story number twelve . . . the "Laughter of Children" story . . . again . . .

LEO's VOICE I will be forty-two years old . . .

MURRAY (*To* ARNOLD; *painfully, pleading*) Arnie . . .

LEO's VOICE And maybe it's the silliest, phoniest, cop-out thing . . .

LEO's VOICE and MURRAY (*In unison*) . . . you ever heard, but the Chipmunk, Chuckles, the little guy I pretend to be, is real to me . . .

LEO's VOICE . . . as real to me as . . . as this phone in my hand; those children, don't ask me why, God I don't know, but they believe in that little fellah . . . (MURRAY *looks up from the floor now and over at the speaker-phone, which is on the other side of the room; his eyes are fixed on it*) Look, Murr', I do what I can for the cash-monies; but also, and I say it without embarrassment, I just love kids, the laughter of children, and we can't have you foolin' with that, Murr', can't have you jokin' . . . (MURRAY *stands up, still looking at the speaker-phone*) because it's this whole, bright, wild sorta child kinda thing . . . (MURRAY *is walking slowly toward the speaker-phone now;* ARNOLD, *watching* MURRAY, *starts to rise from his chair*) it's this very up feeling, it's all young, and you can't joke with it; the laughter of children; those warm waves, that fresh, open, spontaneous laughter, you can feel it on your face . . .

MURRAY (*Picking the speaker-phone up off the desk*) Like a sunburn . . .

LEO'S VOICE Like a sunburn . . .

ARNOLD (*Coming toward* MURRAY *as if to stop him*) Murray . . . wait . . .

LEO'S VOICE And it's a pride thing . . . (MURRAY *turns with the speaker-phone held in his hands and drops it into the wastepaper basket next to the desk. He does this calmly.* ARNOLD, *too late to stop him, stands watching, dumbly paralyzed.* LEO, *unaware, goes right on talking, his voice somewhat garbled and echoing from the bottom of the wastepaper basket*) . . . so then how lovely, how enchanting it is, that I should be paid so well for something I love so much . . . (*Pause*) Say, there's this noise . . . there's this . . . I'm getting this crackling noise on my end here. . . . What's happened to the phone?

ARNOLD (*Sadly, solemnly; looking down into the basket*) Leo, you're in a wastepaper basket.

LEO's VOICE That you, Murray? . . . There's this crackling noise. . . . I can't hear you. . . . Hello? . . . What's going on? . . .

ARNOLD Leo, hold it just a minute, I'll get you.

LEO's VOICE There's this funny noise. . . . Where'd everybody go? Where is everybody? . . . Hello, Murray . . . hello . . . come back . . . come back . . .

ARNOLD (*Fishing amongst the papers in basket for the speaker-phone*) I'll find you, Leo, I'll find you. . . . (*Finally lifts the speaker out of the basket, holds it gently, tenderly in his hands like a child, speaks soothingly to it*) Look, Leo . . . Leo, we had a little . . . some trouble with the phone, we . . . (*Realizes that he is getting no reaction from the box*) Leo? . . . Leo? . . . (*As though the box were a friend whom he thinks might have died, shaking the box tenderly to revive it*) Leo . . . Leo, are you there? . . . Are you there? . . . It's dead. (*Turning to look at* MURRAY, *as though announcing the demise of a dear one*) He's gone.

MURRAY Well, don't look at me like that, Arnie; I didn't *kill* him. He doesn't *live* in that box. . . . Or maybe he does.

ARNOLD A man has a job for you so you drop him in a basket.

84

MURRAY   Arnie, I quit that nonsense five months ago . . .

ARNOLD   Murray, you're a *nut,* a man has a job for you, there's a hearing on Thursday . . .

MURRAY   A fool in a box telling me what's funny, a Welfare Board checking my underwear every week because I don't look good in their files . . . and *I'm* the nut, right? *I'm* the crazy one.

ARNOLD   Murray, you float like a balloon and everybody's waitin' for ya with a pin. I'm trying to put you in *touch,* Murray . . . with *real things;* with . . .

MURRAY   (*Angrily, taking in the office with a sweep of his hand*)   You mean like this office, *real* things, like this office? The world could come to an end and you'd find out about it on the phone. (*Pointing at two framed photographs on* ARNOLD's *desk*)   Pictures of your wife six years ago when she was still a piece, and your kids at their cutest four years ago when they looked best for the office. . . . Oh, you're in *touch* all right, Arnie.

ARNOLD   (*Softly, soothing*)   Murray, you're just a little excited, that's all, just relax, everything's gonna be fine . . .

MURRAY   (*Shouting*)   Damn it . . . get angry; I just insulted you, personally, about your wife, your kids; I just said lousy things to you. Raise your voice, at least your eyebrows . . . (*Pleading painfully*)   Please, have an argument with me . . .

ARNOLD   (*Coaxing*)   We'll call Leo back, we'll apologize to him . . . (MURRAY *goes to the end table, picks up an apple from the bowl of fruit*) Everything's gonna be just fine, Murray, you'll see . . . just fine.

MURRAY Arnie?

ARNOLD Huh?

MURRAY Catch.
 (*Tosses the apple underhand across the room.* ARNOLD *catches it.* MURRAY *exits*)

ARNOLD (*His hand out from catching the apple*) Aw, Murray . . . (*Lowers his hand to his side; speaks quietly, alone now in the office*) Murray, I swear to you, King Kong is *not* on top of the Time-Life Building . . .
 (ARNOLD *discovers the apple in his hand; bites into it. The lights fade quickly. As they dim, we hear* NICK *humming and whistling "Yes, Sir, That's My Baby." The lights go up on* MURRAY's *apartment.* NICK's *humming and whistling fades back so that it is coming from outside the window; the humming grows louder again after a second or two as, it would seem, he descends the fire-escape ladder from Mrs. Myers' apartment. It is early evening. No one is onstage. The apartment has been rather spectacularly rehabilitated by* SANDRA *since we saw it last. The great clutter of* MURRAY's *nonsense collection, clocks, radios, knickknacks, has been cleared away, the books have been neatly arranged in the bookcases, a hat rack has been placed above the bureau and* MURRAY's *hats are placed neatly on it. There are bright new bedspreads on the two beds and brightly colored throw pillows, one new curtain is already up at the windows and a piece of*

86

*matching material is over the Morris chair. The beach
chair and swivel chair are gone and the wicker chair has
been painted gold, the table has a bright new cloth over
it. Pots of flowers are on the table, the bookshelves, the
file cabinets, headboard and desk; and geraniums are in
a holder hanging from the window molding. The whole
place has been dusted and polished and gives off a bright
glow. After two lines or so of the song,* NICK *enters
through the window from the fire escape, carrying his
pajamas and school books.* NICK *sees the new curtain first,
and then, from his position on the window seat, sees the
other changes in the apartment and smiles appreciatively.*
SANDRA *enters from the kitchen, carrying a mixing bowl
and a spoon. She smiles, glad to see* NICK)

SANDRA   Hello, Nick . . .

NICK   Hello, lady. I came in from the fire escape. Mrs. Myers
lives right upstairs. I went there after school, I . . . (*Indicating her work on the apartment*) Did . . . did you do all
this?

SANDRA   Yes, Nick; do you like it?

NICK (*Goes to her, smiling*)   I think it's superb. I mean, imagine my surprise when I saw it. (*Pause*)   Where's Murray?

SANDRA (*Happily telling him the good news*)   Nick . . . Murray went downtown to see your Uncle Arnold. He's going
to get a job.

NICK   That's terrific. Hey, that's just terrific. (SANDRA *goes to
the folded new curtains on the bed, sits down on the bed, un-*

87

folds one of the curtains, begins attaching curtain hooks and rings to it; NICK *sits next to her, helping her as they talk together*) See, lady, he was developing into a bum. You don't want to see somebody you like developing into a bum, and doing nutty things, right? You know what he does? He hollers. Like we were on Park Avenue last Sunday, it's early in the morning and nobody is in the street, see, there's just all those big quiet apartment houses; and he hollers "Rich people, I want to see you all out on the street for volley ball! Let's snap it up!" And sometimes, if we're in a crowded elevator some place, he turns to me and yells "Max, there'll be no *more* of this self-pity! You're forty, it's time you got *used* to being a midget!" And everybody stares. And he has a wonderful time. What do you do with somebody who hollers like that? Last week in Macy's he did that. (*He laughs*) If you want to know the truth, it was pretty funny. (SANDRA *smiles*) I think you're a very nice lady.

SANDRA Thank you, Nick.

NICK What do you think of me?

SANDRA I think you're very nice also.

NICK A very nice quality you have is that you are a good listener, which is important to me because of how much I talk. (*She laughs, enjoying him*) Hey, you're some laugher, aren't you, lady?

SANDRA I guess so, Nick.

NICK (*Trying to make her feel at home*) Would you like some fruit? An orange maybe?

88

SANDRA   No thank you, Nick.

NICK   If you want to call your mother or something, I mean, feel free to use the telephone . . . or my desk if you want to read a book or something . . . or *any* of the chairs . . .

SANDRA   I will, Nick, thank you.

NICK   O.K. (*Pause*)   Are you going to be staying around here for a while?

SANDRA   I might, yes.

NICK   (*He rises, picks up the pajamas and books he brought in with him; indicates apartment*)   Has . . . has Murray seen . . . all this?

SANDRA   No, not yet.

NICK   (*Nods*)   Not yet. Well . . . (*Goes to the window, steps up on window seat*)   Good luck, lady.
(*He exits through the window, carrying his pajamas and school books, goes back up the fire escape.* SANDRA *crosses to window seat, smiling to herself.* MURRAY *enters, unnoticed by her*)

MURRAY   (*Standing still at the front door, glancing around at the apartment; to himself*)   Oh God, I've been attacked by the *Ladies Home Journal.*
(SANDRA *hears him, goes to him happily*)

SANDRA   Murray, what a nice suit you bought. How is everything, which job did . . .

MURRAY (*Looking around at her work on the apartment*) Hey, look at this. You've started to get rid of the Edgar Allan Poe atmosphere.

SANDRA Don't you like it?

MURRAY (*Looking around, noticing his knickknacks are missing*) Sure. Sure. Lotta work. Place has an unusual quality now. Kind of Fun Gothic.

SANDRA Well, of course I'm really not done yet, the curtains aren't all up, and this chair won't look so bad if we reupholster . . . Come on, Murray, don't keep me in suspense, which one of the jobs did you . . .

MURRAY (*Takes her arm, smiles, seats her on the chair in front of him*) I shall now leave you breathless with the strange and wondrous tale of this sturdy lad's adventures today in downtown Oz. (*She is cheered by his manner and ready to listen*) Picture, if you will, me. I am walking on East Fifty-first Street an hour ago and I decided to construct and develop a really decorative, general-all-purpose apology. Not complicated, just the words "I am sorry," said with a little style.

SANDRA Sorry for what?

MURRAY Anything. For being late, early, stupid, asleep, silly, alive . . . (*He moves about now, acting out the scene on the street for her*) Well, y'know when you're walking down the street talking to yourself how sometimes you suddenly say a coupla words out loud? So I said, "I'm sorry," and this fella, complete stranger, he looks up a second and says, "That's all right, Mac," and goes right on. (MURRAY *and* SANDRA *laugh*) He automatically forgave me. I communicated. Five-o'clock rush-hour in midtown you could say, "Sir, I believe your hair is on fire," and they wouldn't hear you. So I decided to test the whole thing out scientifically, I stayed right there on the corner of Fifty-first and Lex for a while, just saying "I'm sorry" to everybody that went by. (*Abjectly*) "Oh, I'm so sorry, sir . . ." (*Slowly, quaveringly*) "I'm terribly sorry, madam . . ." (*Warmly*) "Say there, miss, I'm sorry." Of course, some people just gave me a funny look, but Sandy, I swear, seventy-five percent of them *forgave* me. (*Acting out the people for her*) "Forget it, buddy" . . . "That's O.K., really." Two ladies forgave me in unison, one fella forgave me from a passing car, and one guy forgave me for his dog. "Poofer forgives the nice man, don't you, Poofer?" Oh, Sandy, it was fabulous. I had tapped some vast reservoir. Something had happened to all of them for which they felt *some*body should apologize. If you went up to people on the street and offered them money, they'd refuse it. But everybody accepts apology immediately. It is the most negotiable currency. I said to them, "I am sorry." And they were all so generous, so kind. You could give 'em love and it wouldn't be accepted half as graciously, as unquestioningly . . .

SANDRA (*Suspiciously, her amusement fading*) That's certainly . . . that's very interesting, Murray.

MURRAY Sandy, I could run up on the roof right now and holler, "I am sorry," and half a million people would holler right back, "That's O.K., just see that you don't do it again!"

SANDRA (*After a pause*) Murray, you didn't take any of the jobs.

MURRAY (*Quietly*) Sandy, I took whatever I am and put a suit on it and gave it a haircut and took it outside and that's what happened. I know what I said this morning, what I promised, and Sandra, I'm sorry, I'm very sorry. (*She just sits there before him and stares at him expressionlessly*) Damn it, lady, that was a beautiful apology. You gotta love a guy who can apologize so nice. I rehearsed for over an hour. (*She just looks at him*) That's the most you should expect from life, Sandy, a really good apology for all the things you won't get.

SANDRA Murray, I don't understand. What happens to Nick? What about the Welfare Board?

MURRAY (*He takes her hand*) Sandra . . .

SANDRA I mean, if you don't like the jobs your brother found for you, then take *any* job . . .

MURRAY (*He takes both of her hands and kneels next to her chair*) Oh, Sandy . . . (*Softly, pleading for her to understand*) Nick, he's a wonderful kid, but he's brought the God-damned world in on me. Don't you understand, Sandy, they'd be checking up on me every week; being judged by people I don't know and who don't know me, a committee of ghosts; gimme a month of that and I'd turn into an ash tray, a bowl of corn flakes, I wouldn't know me on the street. . . . (*Looks under chair*) Have you seen Murray? He was here just a minute ago. . . . (*Looks at her, smiles*)

Hey, have you see Murray? (*Pleading for her to understand*)
I wouldn't be of any use to Nick or you or anybody . . .
(SANDRA *moves away from him, goes to the window seat,
leaves him kneeling at the chair. She is still holding the
curtain she had been working on*)

SANDRA (*Quietly*) I've had no effect on you at all. I've made
no difference. You have no idea what it feels like to have no
effect on people. I am not a leader. I scored very low in
leadership in three different vocational aptitude tests. When
I point my finger, people go the other way . . .
(*Absently, she begins to fold the curtain neatly in her
lap*)

MURRAY   Sandra . . .

SANDRA   In grad school they put me in charge of the Struc-
tured-Childs-Play-Analysis session one day . . . (*She shrugs*)
and all the children fell asleep. I am not a leader.

MURRAY (*Going to her at the window seat; warmly, with love*)
Oh, Sandy, you are a cute, jolly lady . . . please understand.

SANDRA   When you left this morning, I was so sure . . .

MURRAY   This morning . . . (*He sits next to her on the window seat, his arm around her, his free hand gesturing expan-
sively, romantically*)   Oh, Sandy, I saw the most beautiful
sailing this morning . . . The *Sklardahl*, Swedish liner,
bound for Europe. It's a great thing to do when you're about
to start something new; you see a boat off. It's always wonderful; there's a sailing practically every day this time of year.
Sandy, you go down and stand at the dock with all the well-
wishers and throw confetti and make a racket with them.

93

. . . Hey, bon voyage, Charley, have a wonderful time. . . .
It gives you a genuine feeling of the beginning of things.
. . . There's another one Friday, big French ship, two
stacker . . .

> (SANDRA *has been watching him coldly during this*
> *speech; she speaks quietly; catching him in mid-air*)

SANDRA Nick will have to go away now, Murray. (*She looks
away from him*) I bought new bedspreads at Altman's, I
haven't spoken to my mother in two days, and you went to
see a boat off. (*She pauses; then smiles to herself for a moment*) My goodness; I'm a listmaker. (*She leaves him alone
in the window seat*) I have to have enough sense to leave
you, Murray. I can see why Nick liked it here. I would like it
here too if I was twelve years old.

> (*She puts the folded curtain down on a chair, picks up
> her jacket*)

MURRAY (*Coming toward her, warmly*) Come on, stick with
me, Dr. Markowitz, anything can happen above an abandoned Chinese restaurant. . . .

SANDRA (*Looking directly at him; quietly*) Maybe you're won-
derfully independent, Murray, or maybe, maybe you're the
most extraordinarily selfish person I've ever met.

> (*She picks up her hand bag and starts toward the door*)

MURRAY (*Tired of begging; angrily, as she walks toward the
door*) What're you gonna do now, go back and live in a
closet? It's really gonna be quite thrilling, you and Albert,
guarding the Lincoln Tunnel together.

94

SANDRA (*Turning at the door to look at him*) I think, Murray, that you live in a much, much larger closet than I do.

MURRAY (*Painfully*) Lady, lady, please don't look at me like that . . .

SANDRA (*Looking about the apartment; very quietly*) Oh, there are so many really attractive things you can do with a one-room apartment if you're willing to use your imagination. (*Opens the door*) Good-bye, Murray.
> (*She exits.* MURRAY *stands still for a moment; then rushes forward to the closed door, angrily*)

MURRAY (*Shouting*) Hey, damn it, you forgot your files! (*Picks up her files from the bureau, opens the door; but she is gone*) The management is not responsible for personal property! (*Closes the door, puts the files back on the bureau; stands at the door, looking around at the apartment*) And what the hell did you do to my apartment? Where are my clocks? What'd you do with my stuff? Where's my radios? (*His back to the audience, shouting*) What've we got here; God damn Sunnybrook Farm?! What happened to my place? (*Suddenly realizing he is still wearing a new suit, he pulls off his suit jacket, rolls it up into a tight ball, and throws it violently across the room. A moment; then he relaxes, walks casually to the window, puts his favorite hat on, sits, leans back comfortably in the window seat and smiles. He talks out of the window in a loud mock-serious voice*) Campers . . . the entertainment committee was quite disappointed by the really poor turn-out at this morning's community sing. I mean, where's all that old Camp Chickawattamee spirit? Now, I'd like to say that I . . . (*He hesitates;*

95

he can't think of anything to say. A pause; then he haltingly tries again) I'd like to say right now that I . . . that . . . that I . . . (*His voice is soft, vague; he pulls his knees up, folds his arms around them, his head bent on his knees; quietly)* Campers, I can't think of anything to say . . .

(*A moment; then*)

Curtain

ACT THREE

ACT THREE

In the darkness, before the curtain goes up, we hear an old recording of a marching band playing "Stars and Stripes Forever." This goes on rather loudly for a few moments. The music diminishes somewhat as the curtain goes up; and we see that the music is coming from an old phonograph on the wicker chair near the bed. It's about thirty minutes later and, though much of SANDRA'S *work on the apartment is still apparent, it is obvious that* MURRAY *has been busy putting his place back into its old shape. The curtains are gone, as is the tablecloth and the material on the Morris chair. All the flower pots have been put on top of the file cabinet. The swivel chair and the beach chair are back in view. Cluttered about the room again is much of* MURRAY'S *nonsense collection, clocks, radios, knickknacks and stacks of magazines.*

As the curtain goes up, MURRAY *has just retrieved a stack of magazines, the megaphone and the pirate pistol from the closet where* SANDRA *had put them; and we see him now placing them back around the room carefully, as though they were part of some strict design.* ARNOLD *enters, carrying his attaché case; walks to the beach chair, sits, takes his hat off. The two men do not look at each other. The music continues to play.*

ARNOLD (*After a moment*) I didn't even bring a tangerine with me. That's very courageous if you think about it for a minute. (*Looks over at* MURRAY, *who is not facing him, points at record player*) You wanna turn that music off, please? (*No reply from* MURRAY) Murray, the music; I'm trying to . . . (*No reply from* MURRAY, *so* ARNOLD *puts his attaché case and hat on table, goes quickly to the record player and turns the music off;* MURRAY *turns to look at* ARNOLD) O.K., I'm a little slow. It takes me an hour to get

99

insulted. Now I'm insulted. You walked out of my office. That wasn't a nice thing to do to me, Murray . . . (MURRAY *does not reply*) You came into my office like George God; everybody's supposed to come up and audition for Human Being in front of you. (*Comes over closer to him, takes his arm*) Aw, Murray, today, one day, leave the dragons alone, will ya? And look at the dragons you pick on; Sloan, Leo, me; silly old arthritic dragons, step on a toe and we'll start to cry. Murray, I called Leo back, I apologized, told him my phone broke down; I got him to come over here tonight. He's anxious to see you, everything's O.K. . . .

MURRAY Hey, you just never give up, do you, Arnie?

ARNOLD Listen to me, Murray, do I ever tell you what to do . . .

MURRAY Yes, all the time.

ARNOLD If you love this kid, then you gotta take any kinda stupid job to keep him . . .

MURRAY Now you're an expert on love.

ARNOLD Not an expert, but I sure as hell value my amateur standing. Murray, about him leaving, have you told him yet?

MURRAY (*Softly; realizing* ARNOLD'S *genuine concern*) Arnie, don't worry, I know how to handle it. I've got a coupla days to tell him. And don't underrate Nick, he's gonna understand this a lot better than you think.

ARNOLD Murray, I finally figured out your problem. There's only one thing that really bothers you . . . (*With a sweep of his hand*) Other people. (*With a mock-secretive tone*) If it wasn't for them other people, everything would be great, huh, Murray? I mean, you think everything's fine, and then you go out into the street . . . and there they all *are* again, right? The Other People; taking up space, bumping into you, asking for things, making lines to wait on, taking cabs away from ya . . . The Enemy . . . Well, *watch* out, Murray, they're *every*where . . .

MURRAY Go ahead, Arnie, give me advice, at thirty thousand a year you can afford it.

ARNOLD Oh, I get it, if I'm so smart why ain't I poor? You better get a damn good act of your own before you start giving *mine* the razzberry. What's this game you play gonna be like ten years from now, without youth? Murray, Murray, I can't *watch* this, you gotta *shape* up . . .

MURRAY (*Turning quickly to face* ARNOLD; *in a surprised tone*) Shape *up*? (*Looks directly at* ARNOLD; *speaks slowly*) Arnie, what the hell happened to you? You got so old. I don't know you any more. When you quit "Harry the Fur King" on Thirty-eighth Street, remember?

ARNOLD That's twenty years ago, Murray.

MURRAY You told me you were going to be in twenty businesses in twenty years if you had to, till you found out what you wanted. Things were always going to change. Harry said you were not behaving maturely enough for a salesman; your clothes didn't match or something . . . (*Laughs in affectionate memory of the event*) So the next day, you dressed perfectly, homburg, gray suit, cuff links, carrying a briefcase and a rolled umbrella . . . and you came into

Harry's office on roller skates. You weren't going to take crap from *any*body. So that's the business you finally picked . . . taking crap from *every*body.

ARNOLD I don't do practical jokes any more, if that's what you mean . . .

MURRAY (*Grabs both of* ARNOLD's *arms tensely*) Practical, that's right; a way to stay alive. If most things aren't funny, Arn, then they're only exactly what they are; then it's one long dental appointment interrupted occasionally by something exciting, like waiting or falling asleep. What's the point if I leave everything exactly the way I find it? Then I'm just adding to the noise, then I'm just taking up some more room on the subway.

ARNOLD Murray, the Welfare Board has these specifications; all you have to do is meet a couple specifications . . .
    (MURRAY *releases his grip on* ARNOLD's *arms;* MURRAY's *hands drop to his sides*)

MURRAY Oh, Arnie, you don't understand any more. You got that wide stare that people stick in their eyes so nobody'll know their head's asleep. You got to be a shuffler, a moaner. You want me to come sit and eat fruit with you and watch the clock run out. You start to drag and stumble with the rotten weight of all the people who should have been told off, all the things you should have said, all the specifications that aren't yours. The only thing you got left to reject is your food in a restaurant if they do it wrong and you can send it back and make a big fuss with the waiter. . . . (MURRAY *turns away from* ARNOLD, *goes to the window seat, sits down*) Arnold, five months ago I forgot what *day* it was. I'm on the subway on my way to work and I didn't know what day it was and it scared the hell out of me. . . . (*Quietly*) I was sitting in the express looking out the window same as every morning watching the local stops go by in the dark with an empty head and my arms folded, not feeling great and not feeling rotten, just not feeling, and for a minute I couldn't remember, I didn't know, unless I really concentrated, whether it was a Tuesday or a Thursday . . . or a . . . for a minute it could have been *any* day, Arnie . . . sitting in the train going through any day . . . in the dark through any year. . . . Arnie, it scared the hell out of me. (*Stands up*) You got to know what day it is. You got to know what's the name of the game and what the rules are with nobody else telling you. You have to own your days and name them, each one of them, every one of them, or else the years go right by and none of them belong to you. (*Turns to look at* ARNOLD) And that ain't just for weekends, kiddo . . . (*Looks at* ARNOLD *a moment longer, then speaks in a pleasant tone*) Here it is, the day after Irving R. Feldman's birthday, for God's sake . . . (*Takes a hat, puts it on*) And I never even congratulated him . . .

> (*Starts to walk briskly toward the front door.* ARNOLD *shouts in a voice stronger than we have ever heard from him*)

ARNOLD Murray!

> (MURRAY *stops, turns, startled to hear this loud a voice from* ARNOLD. ARNOLD *looks fiercely at* MURRAY *for a moment, then* ARNOLD *too looks surprised, starts to laugh*)

MURRAY What's so funny?

ARNOLD Wow, I scared myself. You hear that voice? Look at

that, I got you to stop, I got your complete, full attention, the floor is mine now . . . (*Chuckles awkwardly*) And I can't think of a God-damned thing to say . . . (*Shrugs his shoulders; picks up his hat from the table*) I have long been aware, Murray . . . I have long been aware that you don't respect me much. . . . I suppose there are a lot of brothers who don't get along. . . . But in reference . . . to us, considering the factors . . . (*Smiles, embarrassed*) Sounds like a contract, doesn't it? (*Picks up his briefcase, comes over to* MURRAY) Unfortunately for you, Murray, you want to be a hero. Maybe if a fella falls into a lake, you can jump in and save him; there's still that kind of stuff. But who gets opportunities like that in midtown Manhattan, with all that traffic. (*Puts on his hat*) I am willing to deal with the available world and I do not choose to shake it up but to live with it. There's the people who spill things, and the people who get spilled on; I do not choose to notice the stains, Murray. I have a wife and I have children, and business, like they say, is business. I am not an exceptional man, so it is possible for me to stay with things the way they are. I'm lucky. I'm gifted. I have a talent for surrender. I'm at peace. But you are cursed; and I like you so it makes me sad, you don't have the gift; and I see the torture of it. All I can do is worry for you. But I will not worry for myself; you cannot convince me that I am one of the Bad Guys. I get up, I go, I lie a little, I peddle a little, I watch the rules, I talk the talk. We fellas have those offices high up there so we can catch the wind and go with it, however it blows. But, and I will not apologize for it, I take pride; I am the best possible Arnold Burns. (*Pause*) Well . . . give my regards to Irving R. Feldman, will ya?

(*He starts to leave*)

MURRAY (*Going toward him*) Arnold . . .

ARNOLD Please, Murray . . . (*Puts his hand up*) Allow me once to leave a room before you do.

> (ARNOLD *snaps on record player as he walks past it to the front door; he exits.* MURRAY *goes toward the closed door, the record player has warmed up and we suddenly hear "Stars and Stripes Forever" blaring loudly from the machine again;* MURRAY *turns at this sound and stands for a long moment looking at the record player as the music comes from it.* NICK *enters through the window from the fire escape, unnoticed by* MURRAY. NICK *looks about, sees that the apartment is not quite what it was an hour before*)

NICK Hey, Murray . . .

MURRAY (*Turns, sees* NICK) Nick . . .
> (*Turns the record player off; puts the record on the bed*)

NICK Hey, where's the lady?

MURRAY Well, she's not here right now . . .

NICK (*Stepping forward to make an announcement*) Murray, I have decided that since *you* are getting a job today then I made up my mind it is time for *me* also to finish a certain matter which I have been putting off.

MURRAY Nick, listen, turned out the only job I could get in a hurry was with Chuckles . . .

NICK (*Nodding in approval*) Chuckles, huh? Well, fine. (*Then, grimly*) Just as long as I don't have to watch that terrible program every morning. (*Returning to his announcement*) For many months now I have been concerned with a decision, Murray . . . Murray, you're not listening.

MURRAY (*Distracted*) Sure I'm listening, yeah . . .

NICK The past couple months I have been thinking about different names and considering different names because in four weeks I'm gonna be thirteen and I gotta pick my permanent name, like we said.

MURRAY Why don't you just go on calling yourself Nick? You've been using it the longest.

NICK Nick is a name for a short person. And since I am a short person I do not believe I should put a lot of attention on it.

MURRAY Whaddya mean, where'd you get the idea you were short?

NICK From people who are taller than I am.

MURRAY That's ridiculous.

NICK Sure, standing up there it's ridiculous, but from down here where I am it's not so ridiculous. And half the girls in my class are taller than me. Especially Susan Bookwalter. (NICK *sits dejectedly in the swivel chair*)

MURRAY (*Crouching over next to him*) Nick, you happen to be a nice medium height for your age.

NICK (*Pointing at* MURRAY) Yeah, so how is it everybody crouches over a little when I'm around?

MURRAY (*Straightening up*) Because you're a kid. (*Sits next to him*) Listen, you come from a fairly tall family. Next couple years you're gonna grow like crazy. Really, Nick, every day you're getting bigger.

NICK So is Susan Bookwalter. (*Stands*) So for a couple of months I considered various tall names. Last month I considered, for a while, Zachery, but I figured there was a chance Zachery could turn into a short, fat, bald name. Then I thought about Richard, which is not really tall, just very thin with glasses. Then last week I finally, really, decided and I took out a new library card to see how it looks and today I figured I would make it definite and official.
      (*He takes a library card out of his pocket, hands it to* MURRAY)

MURRAY (*Looks at the card, confused*) This is *my* library card.

NICK No, that's the whole thing; it's mine.

MURRAY But it says *"Murray* Burns" on it . . .

NICK Right, that's the name I picked. So I took out a new card to see how it looks and make it official.

MURRAY (*Looks at the card, is moved and upset by it, but covers with cool dignity; stands, speaks very formally*) Well, Nick, I'm flattered . . . I want you to know that I'm . . . very flattered by this. (NICK *goes to the alcove to put his school books and pajamas away*) Well, why the hell did you . . . I mean, damn it, Nick, that's too many Murrays, very confusing . . . (MURRAY *begins to shift the card awkwardly from one hand to the other, speaks haltingly*) Look, why don't you call yourself George, huh? Very strong name there, George . . .

NICK (*Shaking his head firmly*) No. We made a deal it was up to me to pick which name and that's the name I decided on; "Murray."

MURRAY Well, what about Jack? What the hell's wrong with Jack? Jack Burns . . . sounds like a promising heavyweight.

NICK I like the name I picked better.

MURRAY (*Very quietly*) Or Martin . . . or Robert . . .

NICK Those names are all square.

LEO'S VOICE (*From behind the door, shouting*) Is this it? Is this the Lion's Den, here? Hey, Murr'!

MURRAY (*Softly*) Ah, I hear the voice of a chipmunk.

NICK (*Going into the bathroom*) I better go put on a tie.

MURRAY (*Goes to the door; stands there a moment, looks over to the other side of the room at* NICK, *who is offstage in the bathroom; smiles, speaks half to himself, very softly*) You coulda called yourself Charlie. Charlie is a very musical name.
    (*Then, he opens the door.* LEO HERMAN *enters. He wears a camel's-hair coat and hat. The coat, like his suit, is a little too big for him. He is carrying a paper bag and a large Chuckles statue—a life-size cardboard cutout of himself in his character of Chuckles the Chipmunk; the statue wears a blindingly ingratiating smile*)

LEO (*With great enthusiasm*) Murray, there he is! There's the old monkey! There's the old joker, right?

MURRAY (*Quietly, smiling politely*) Yeah, Leo, here he is. (*Shakes* LEO's *hand*) It's . . . it's very nice to see you again, Leo, after all this time.

LEO (*Turning to see* NICK, *who has come out of the bathroom wearing his tie*) There he is! There's the little guy! (*Goes to* NICK *carrying the statue and the paper bag*) Looka here, little guy . . . (*Setting the statue up against the wall next to the window*) I gotta Chuckles statue for you.

NICK (*With his best company manners*) Thank you, Mr. Herman; imagine how pleased I am to receive it. It's a very artistic statue and very good cardboard too.

LEO (*Taking a Chuckles hat from the paper bag; a replica of the furry, big-eared hat worn by the statue*) And I gotta Chuckles hat for you too, just like the old Chipmunk wears. (*He puts the hat on* NICK's *head*)

NICK Thank you.

LEO (*Crouching over to* NICK's *height*) Now that you've got the Chuckles hat, you've got to say the Chuckles-hello.

NICK (*Confused, but anxious to please*) The what?

LEO (*Prompting him*) "Chip-chip, Chippermunkie!" (*He salutes*)

NICK Oh, yeah . . . "Chip-chip, Chippermunkie!" (*He salutes too*)

LEO May I know your name?

NICK It's Nick, most of the time.

LEO Most of the . . . (*Pulling two bags of potato chips from his overcoat pockets*) Say, look what I've got, two big bags of Chuckle-Chip potato chips! How'd ya like to put these crispy chips in some bowls or somethin' for us, huh? (NICK *takes the two bags, goes to the kitchen*) And take your time, Nick, your uncle 'n' me have some grown-up talkin' to do. (*After* NICK *exits into the kitchen*) The kid hates me. I can tell. Didn't go over very well with him, pushed a little too hard. He's a nice kid, Murray.

MURRAY How are *your* kids, Leo?

LEO Fine, fine. But, Murray, I swear, even *they* don't like my show since you stopped writing it. My youngest one . . . my six-year-old . . .
(*He can't quite remember*)

MURRAY Ralphie.

LEO Ralphie; he's been watching the Funny Bunny Show now every morning instead of me. (*Begins pacing up and down*) Oh *boy,* have I been bombing out on the show. Murray, do you know what it *feels* like to bomb out in front of children? You flop out in front of kids and, Murray, I swear to God, they're ready to *kill* you. (*Stops pacing*) Or else, they just stare at you, that's the worst, that hurt, innocent stare like you just killed their pup or raped their turtle or something. (*Goes over to* MURRAY) Murray, to have you back with me on the show, to see you at the studio again tomorrow, it's gonna be *beautiful.* You're the *best.*

Jason Robards, Jr., and Gene Saks, as MURRAY BURNS and
LEO HERMAN

MURRAY I appreciate your feeling that way, Leo.

LEO This afternoon, Murray, on the phone, you hung up on me, didn't you?

MURRAY I'm sorry Leo, I was just kidding . . . I hope you . . .

LEO (*Sadly*) Murray, why do you do that to me? Aw, don't tell me, I know, I make people nervous. Who can listen to me for ten minutes? (*Begins pacing up and down again, strokes his tie*) See *that*? See how I keep touching my suit and my tie? I keep touching myself to make sure I'm still there. Murray, I get this feeling, maybe I vanished when I wasn't looking.

MURRAY Oh, I'm sure that you're here, Leo.

LEO (*Pointing at* MURRAY) See how he talks to me? A little nasty. (*Smiles suddenly*) Well, I like it. It's straight and it's real and I like it. You know what I got around me on the show? Finks, dwarfs, phonies and frogs. No Murrays. The show: boring, boredom, bore . . . (*Cups his hands around his mouth and shouts*) boring, boring . . .
     (*During these last few words,* SANDRA *has entered through the partly open door.* MURRAY *turns, sees her.*)

SANDRA (*Staying near the doorway; reserved, official*) Murray, I believe that I left my files here; I came to get my files; may I have my files, please. I . . . (*She sees* LEO, *comes a few feet into the room*) Oh, excuse me . . .

MURRAY (*Cordially, introducing them*) Chuckles the Chipmunk . . . this is Minnie Mouse.

LEO (*Absently*) Hi, Minnie . . .

SANDRA (*Looking from one to the other, taking in the situation, smiles; to* LEO) You must be . . . you must be Mr. Herman.

LEO (*Mumbling to himself*) Yeah, I must be. I must be him; I'd rather not be, but what the hell . . .

SANDRA (*Smiling, as she turns right around and goes to the door*) Well, I'll be on my way . . .
  (*She exits.* MURRAY *picks up her files from the bureau, goes to the door with them*)

LEO (*Interrupting* MURRAY *on his way to the door*) Very attractive girl, that Minnie; what does she do?

MURRAY She's my decorator.

LEO (*Looking around the apartment*) Well, she's done a *wonderful* job! (*Indicating the apartment with a sweep of his hand*) This place is great. It's loose, it's open, it's free. Love it. Wonderful, crazy place. My God . . . you must make out like mad in this place, huh? (MURRAY *closes door, puts the files back on the bureau;* LEO *is walking around the apartment*) How come I never came here before?

MURRAY You were here last January, Leo.

LEO Funny thing, work with me for three years and I never saw your apartment.

MURRAY You were here last January, Leo.

LEO (*Stops pacing, turns to* MURRAY) Wait a minute, wait a
minute, wasn't I here recently, in the winter? Last January,
I think . . . (*Goes over to* MURRAY) Oh, I came here to get
you back on the show and you wouldn't listen, you went into
the kitchen, sang "Yes, Sir, That's My Baby." I left feeling
very foolish, like I had footprints on my face. . . . You old
monkey. (*Smiles, musses up* MURRAY's *hair*) You're an old
monkey, aren't ya? (*Starts pacing again*) You know what
I got from that experience? A rash. I broke out something terrible. . . . Minnie Mouse! (*Stops pacing*) Minnie
Mouse! (*Laughs loudly, points at the door*) You told me
her name was Minnie Mouse! I swear to God, Murray, I
think my mission in life is to feed you straight-lines . . .
(*Taking in the apartment with a sweep of his hand*) It's
kind of a fall-out shelter, that's what you got here, Murr',
protection against the idiots in the atmosphere. Free, freer,
freest . . . (*Cups his hands around his mouth, shouts*)
Free! Free! (*Takes off his coat*) Another year and I'm
gonna cut loose from the God-damn Chipmunk show. Binds
me up, hugs me. Finks, dwarfs, phonies and frogs . . .
(*Following* MURRAY *to the window seat*) Two of us should
do something new, something wild; new kind of kid's show,
for adults maybe . . .

MURRAY (*Sitting on the window seat*) You told me the same
thing three years ago, Leo.

LEO (*Sits next to* MURRAY) Well, whaddya want from me?
I'm a coward; everybody knows that. (*Suddenly seeing the
Chuckles statue against the wall next to him*) Oh God!
(*Points at the statue; in anguish*) Did you ever see any-
thing so *immodest?* I bring a big statue of myself as a gift
for a child! I mean, the *pure ego* of it . . . (*Covers his face*

with his hands) I am ashamed. Murray, could you throw a sheet over it or something . . . (*Sees* NICK, *who has just come out of the kitchen with two bowls of potato chips*) Mmmm, good! Here they are. (*Grabs one bowl from* NICK'S *hand, gives it to* MURRAY. *Then* LEO *turns to* NICK, *assumes the character and the voice of Chuckles the Chipmunk; a great mock-frown on his face, he goes into a routine for* NICK) Oh, goshes, kidderoonies, look at your poor Chippermunk friend; he got his mouff stuck. No matter how hard I try I can't get my mouth unstuck. But maybe—if you Chippermunks yell, "Be happy, Chuckles," maybe then it'll get unstuck . . . (LEO *waits.* NICK *does not react.* LEO *prompts* . NICK *in a whisper*) You're supposed to yell, "Be happy, Chuckles."

NICK Oh, yeah . . . sure . . . (*Glances quickly at* MURRAY; *then, a little embarrassed, he yells*) Be happy, Chuckles!

LEO Oh *boy!* (*His frown changes to a giant smile*) You *fixed* me! Looka my mouff! (*He jumps up in the air*) Now I'm all fixed!
    (*Gets no reaction from* NICK. NICK *stands patiently in front of* LEO)

NICK (*Offering the other bowl of potato chips to* LEO, *trying to be polite*) Mr. Herman, don't you want your . . .

LEO (*Not accepting the potato chips, speaking in his own voice again, stroking his tie nervously*) That was a bit from tomorrow morning's show. You'll know it ahead of all the kids in the neighborhood.

NICK Thank you.

LEO   That . . . that was one of the funny parts there, when I couldn't move my mouth.

NICK   Yeah?

LEO   Didn't you think it was funny?

NICK   Yeah, that was pretty funny.

LEO   (*Smiling nervously*)   Well, don't you laugh or something when you see something funny?

NICK   It just took me by surprise is all. So I didn't get a chance. (*Offering him the potato chips, politely*)   Here's your . . .

LEO   Another funny part was when I jumped up with the smile there, at the end there. That was another one.

NICK   Uh-huh.

LEO   (*Pressing on, beginning to get tense*)   And the finish on the bit, see, I've got the smile . . . (NICK, *looking trapped, stands there as* LEO *switches back to his Chipmunk voice and puts a giant smile on his face*)   Now I'm aaaall fixed, Chippermunks! (*Sudden mock-pathos in his eyes*)   Oooops! *Now* I got stuck the *other* way! Oh, *oh*, now my face is stuck the *other* way!

> (*Throws up his arms, does a loose-legged slapstick fall back onto the floor. Remains prone, waiting for* NICK's *reaction.* NICK *stands there looking at* LEO *quite solemnly*)

NICK   (*Nods his head up and down approvingly*)   That's terrific, Mr. Herman. (*With admiration*)   That's all you have to do, you just get up and do that and they pay you and everything.

LEO You didn't laugh.

NICK I was waiting for the funny part.

LEO (*Sits up*) That was the funny part.

NICK Oh, when you fell down on the . . .

LEO When I fell down on the floor here.

NICK See, the thing is, I was . . .

LEO (*Gets up from the floor, paces up and down tensely*) I know, waiting for the funny part. Well, you missed another funny part.

NICK Another one. Hey, I'm really sorry, Mr. Herman, I . . .

LEO Forget it . . . I just happen to know that that bit is very *funny*. I can prove it to you. (*Takes small booklet from pocket, opens it, shows it to* NICK) Now, what does that say there, second line there?

NICK (*Reading from the booklet*) "Frown bit; eighty-five percent of audience; outright prolonged laughter on frown bit."

LEO That's the analysis report the agency did for me on Monday's preview audience. The routine I just did for you, got outright prolonged laughter; eighty-five percent.

MURRAY You could try him on sad parts, Leo; he's very good on sad parts.

LEO (*Goes to* MURRAY *at the window seat, shows him another page in the booklet*) Matter fact, there's this poignant-type bit I did at the Preview Theatre: "Sixty percent of audience; noticeably moved."

MURRAY   They left the theatre?

LEO   (*Tensely, angrily*)   There he is; there's the old joker; Murray the joker, right?

NICK   I do some routines. I can imitate the voice of Alexander Hamilton.

LEO   That's lovely, but I . . .

NICK   I do Alexander Hamilton and Murray does this terrific Thomas Jefferson; we got the voices just right.

MURRAY   (*In a dignified voice; to* NICK)   Hello there, Alex, how are you?

NICK   (*In a dignified voice; to* MURRAY)   Hello there, Tom; say, you should have been in Congress this morning. My goodness, there was quite a discussion on . . .

LEO   Now, that's *ridiculous*. You . . . you can't *do* an imitation of Alexander Hamilton; nobody knows what he *sounds* like . . .

NICK   (*Pointing triumphantly at* LEO)   *That's* the *funny* part.

MURRAY   (*Shaking his head regretfully*)   You missed the funny part, Leo.

LEO   (*Walking away from them*)   I'm getting a terrible rash on my neck. (*Turns to them, growing louder and more tense*

117

with each word) The routine I did for him was *funny*. I was workin' good in front of the kid, I know how to use my God-damn *warmth*, I don't go over with these odd kids; I mean, here I am right in *front* of him, in *person* for God's sake, and he's *staring* at me . . . (*Moves toward them, on the attack*) It's oddness here, Murray, *odd*ness. Alexander *Ham*ilton imitations! Jaded jokes for old men. Murray, what you've done to this kid. It's a damn shame, a child can't enjoy little animals, a damn shame . . . (*Really on the attack now; waving at the apartment, shouting*) The way you brought this kid up, Murray, grotesque atmosphere, *unhealthy,* and you're not even guilty about it, women in and out, *dec*orators; had he been brought up by a *normal* person and not in this *mad*house . . .

NICK (*Quietly, going toward* LEO) Hey, don't say that . . .

LEO A certain kind of freakish way of growing up . . .

NICK (*Quietly*) Hey, are you calling me a freak? You called me a freak. Take back what you said.

LEO (*Walks away from them, mumbling to himself*) On June third I will be forty-two years old and I'm standing here arguing with a twelve-year-old kid . . . (LEO *quiets down, turns, comes toward* NICK, *sits on bed,* NICK *standing next to him; speaks calmly to* NICK) See, Nicky, humor is a cloudy, wonderland thing, but simple and clear like the blue, blue sky. All I want is your simple, honest, child's opinion of my routine; for children are too honest to be wise . . .

NICK (*Looking directly at* LEO, *calmly, quietly, slowly*) My simple, child's reaction to what you did is that you are not funny. Funnier than you is even Stuart Slossman my friend who is eleven and puts walnuts in his mouth and makes noises. What is not funny is to call us names and what is mostly not funny is how sad you are that I would feel sorry for you if it wasn't for how dull you are and those are the worst-tasting potato chips I ever tasted. And that is my opinion from the blue, blue sky.

> (NICK *and* LEO *stay in their positions, looking at each other. A moment; then* MURRAY *throws his head back and laughs uproariously.* LEO *stands; the bowl of potato chips tips over in his hand, the chips spilling onto the floor*)

LEO (*Seeing* MURRAY's *laughter, goes to him at the Morris chair; angrily*) Murray the joker, right? You didn't want to come back to work for me, you just got me up here to step on my face again! (NICK, *unnoticed by* LEO, *has gone quickly into his alcove and comes out now with his ukulele, playing and singing "Yes, Sir, That's My Baby" with great spirit.* LEO, *hearing this, turns to look at* NICK) It's the song. It's the good-*bye* song. (LEO *grabs his hat and coat quickly, as* NICK *goes on playing, starts for front door, shouting*) Getting *out*, bunch of *nuts* here, *crazy* people . . .

MURRAY Leo, wait . . . (*Goes to the door to stop* LEO) Leo, wait . . . I'm sorry . . . wait . . . (LEO *stops at the door;* MURRAY *goes down toward* NICK, *who is near the alcove, still playing the song*) Nick, you better stop now . . .

NICK Come on, Murray, get your uke, we'll sing to him and he'll go away . . .

MURRAY (*Quietly*) Nick, we can't . . . (*Gently taking the uke from* NICK, *puts it on the window seat*) Just put this down, huh?

NICK (*Confused by this; urgently*) Come on, Murray, let him go away, he called us names, we gotta get rid of him . . .

MURRAY Quiet now, Nick . . . just be quiet for a minute . . .
(*Starts to go back toward* LEO)

NICK (*Shouting*) Murray, please let him go away . . . (NICK, *seeing the Chuckles statue next to him against the wall, grabs it angrily, throws it down on the floor*) It's a crummy statue . . . that crummy statue . . . (*Begins to kick the statue fiercely, jumping up and down on it, shouting*) It's a terrible statue, rotten cardboard . . .
(MURRAY *comes quickly back to* NICK, *holds both of his arms, trying to control him*)

MURRAY Aw, Nick, please, no more now, stop it . . .
(*There is a great struggle between them;* NICK *is fighting wildly to free himself from* MURRAY's *arms*)

NICK (*Near tears, shouting*) We don't want jerks like that around here, Murray, let him go away, we gotta get rid of him, Murray, we gotta get rid of him . . .

MURRAY (*Lifts the struggling* NICK *up into his arms, hugging him to stop him*) No, Nick . . . I'm sorry, Nick . . . we can't . . . (NICK *gives up, hangs limply in* MURRAY's *arms.* MURRAY *speaks quietly, with love*) I'm sorry . . . I'm sorry, kid . . . I'm sorry . . .
(*He puts* NICK *down, still holding him*)

NICK (*After a pause; quietly, in disbelief*) Murray . . .

MURRAY You better go to your room.

NICK This is a one-room apartment.

MURRAY Oh. Then go to your alcove. (NICK *waits a moment, then turns, betrayed, walks over to his alcove, lies down on the bed.* MURRAY *looks over at* LEO, *who is standing at the front door. He walks slowly over to* LEO, *looking down at the floor; humbly*) Leo . . . hope you didn't misunderstand . . . we were just kidding you . . . we . . .

LEO (*Coming toward* MURRAY, *apologetically*) I, myself, I got carried away there myself.

MURRAY We all got a little excited, I guess. (*Reaches out to shake* LEO's *hand*) So, I'll see you at work in the morning, Leo.

LEO (*Smiling, shaking* MURRAY's *hand*) Great to have you back, fellah. (*Pause*) You both hate me.

MURRAY Nobody hates you, Leo.

LEO I hollered at the kid, I'm sorry. I didn't mean to cause any upset. I don't get along too good with kids . . .

MURRAY Don't worry about it.

LEO Wanna come have a drink with me, Murray? We could . . .

MURRAY No thanks; maybe another night, Leo.

LEO Look, after I leave, you horse around a little with the kid, he'll feel better.

MURRAY Right, Leo.

LEO (*Pauses; then comes closer to* MURRAY) Murray . . . that bit I did was funny, wasn't it?

MURRAY (*After a moment*) Yeah, Leo . . . I guess it was just a bad day for you.

LEO (*Pointing at the Chuckles statue on the floor; quietly, but giving a command*) You don't want to leave that statue lying around like that, huh, Murray?

MURRAY Oh, no. (*Goes to statue obediently, lifts it up off the floor, leans it upright against the wall*) There.

LEO Fine.

MURRAY See you tomorrow, Leo.

LEO (*Smiles*) Yeah, see ya tomorrow at the studio . . . (*Ruffles up* MURRAY'*s hair*) You old monkey. (*Goes to the door*) Hey, you're an old monkey, aren't you?
  (LEO *exits.* MURRAY *stays at the door for a moment.* NICK *is sitting on the alcove step, his back to* MURRAY)

MURRAY (*Walking over to* NICK, *trying to make peace with him*) Say, I could use a roast-turkey sandwich right now, couldn't you, Nick? On rye, with cole slaw and Russian dressing. . . .
  (NICK *does not reply.* MURRAY *sits down next to him on the alcove step.* NICK *refuses to look at* MURRAY. *They are both silent for a moment*)

NICK Guy calls us names. Guy talks to us like that. Shoulda got rid of that moron. Coulda fooled the Welfare people or something . . . (SANDRA *enters through the partly open door, unnoticed by them; she stays up in the doorway, watching them*) We coulda gone to Mexico or New Jersey or someplace.

MURRAY I hear the delicatessen in Mexico is terrible.

NICK (*After a moment*) I'm gonna call myself *Theodore.*

MURRAY As long as you don't call yourself Beatrice.

NICK O.K., fool around. Wait'll you see a Theodore running around here. (*Silent for a moment, his back still to* MURRAY; *then, quietly*) Another coupla seconds he woulda been out the door . . . (*Turns to look at* MURRAY) Why'd you go chicken on me, Murray? What'd you stop me for?

MURRAY Because your routines give me outright prolonged laughter, Theodore.

SANDRA (*After a pause*) Four ninety-five for this tablecloth and you leave it around like this . . . (*Picks up the discarded tablecloth from the chair*) A perfectly new tablecloth and already there are stains on it . . . (*Sits on the Morris chair, starts to dab at the tablecloth with her handkerchief*) You know, it's very interesting that I left my files here. That I forgot them. I mean, psychologically, if you want to analyze that. Of course, last month I left my handbag in the Automat, and I have no idea what that means at all. (MURRAY *leaves alcove, starts toward her*) I think that the pattern of our relationship, if we examine it, is very intricate, the different areas of it, especially the whole "good-bye" area of it, and also the "hello" and "how-are-you" area . . . of it.

MURRAY (*Standing next to her chair now, smiles warmly*)
Hello, Sandy, and how are you?

SANDRA (*Looks up at him, smiles politely*) Hello, Murray.
(*Goes right back to her work, rubbing the tablecloth with
her handkerchief*) You're standing in my light.

MURRAY Oh.
(*He retreats a step*)

NICK (*Walking over to her*) Hello, lady.

SANDRA Hello, Nick.

NICK (*Indicating her work on the tablecloth*) Lady, can I help
you with any of that?

SANDRA Matter of fact, Nick . . . (*She stands; her arm around
NICK, she goes to center with him*) Nick, I don't think the
effect, I mean, the overall design of this room, is really helped
by all these . . . (*Gesturing to* MURRAY's *stuff around the
bed*) these knickknacks.

NICK You mean the junk?

SANDRA Yes.

NICK Yeah, not too good for the overall design.

SANDRA If you'd just put them away in that carton there.
(*She indicates a carton near the bed*)

NICK Sure, lady . . .

A THOUSAND CLOWNS

(NICK *goes quickly to the carton, begins to put* MURRAY's *junk into it—some radios, a megaphone, some clocks.* SANDRA *starts putting the tablecloth on the table*)

MURRAY (*Realizes that they are taking over, moves forward, trying to halt the proceedings*) Hey, Sandy, now wait a minute . . . (*She goes on with her work, putting a piece of material over the Morris chair. He turns at the sound of one of his radio cabinets being dropped into the carton by* NICK) Listen, Nick, I didn't tell you to . . . Nick . . .

NICK (*Looking up from his work*) Wilbur . . . (*Drops a clock into the carton*) Wilbur Malcolm Burns.
    (SANDRA *is putting the flowers back around the room, picking up the magazines*)

MURRAY (*Protesting*) Hey, now, both of you, will ya wait a minute here, will ya just wait . . . (*They ignore him, going on with their work. He shrugs, defeated; gives up, goes over to the windows, away from them, sits down sadly in the window seat*) Wonder what kind of weather we got out there tonight. (*Looks out of window; as usual, he can see nothing but the gray, blank wall of the building a few feet opposite; sadly, to himself*) Never can see the God-damned weather. We got a permanent fixture out there: twilight in February. Some day that damn building'll fall down into Seventh Avenue so I can see the weather. (*Leans over, begins to talk out of the window*) Everybody onstage for the Hawaiian number, please . . . (SANDRA, *during these last few lines, has gone to the phone, dialed, listened a few moments and hung up.* MURRAY *hears her hang up, turns to her*) What're you doing?

SANDRA I just spoke to the Weather Lady. She says it's a beautiful day.
(*She goes back to her work on the apartment*)

MURRAY (*He continues to talk out the window, softly at first*) Well, then, if you're not ready, we better work on the Military March number. Now the last time we ran this, let's admit it was pretty ragged. I mean, the whole "Spirit of '76" float was in dis*grace*ful shape yesterday . . . O.K. now, let's go, everybody ready . . . (*As* MURRAY *continues to talk out the window,* NICK *looks up from his work, smiles, picks up a record from the bed, puts it on the record player, turns it on*) Grenadiers ready, Cavalry ready, Cossacks ready, Rough Riders ready, Minute Men ready . . . (*The record player has warmed up now and we hear "Stars and Stripes Forever."* MURRAY *hears the music, turns from the window, smiling, acknowledges* NICK'S *assistance; turns to the window again, his voice gradually growing in volume*) O.K. now, let's go . . . ready on the cannons, ready on the floats, ready on the banners, ready on the flags . . . (*The music builds up with* MURRAY'S *voice,* NICK *humming along with the band and* SANDRA *laughing as* MURRAY *shouts*) Let's go . . . let's go . . . let's go . . .
(*His arms are outstretched*)

Curtain